Faces in the Crowd

Reaching Your International Neighbor for Christ

By Donna S. Thomas

NEW HOPE
PUBLISHERS
Birmingham, Alabama

New Hope® Publishers
P.O. Box 12065
Birmingham, AL 35202-2065
www.newhopepublishers.com

New Hope Publishers is a division of WMU®.

Thomas, Donna S., 1928-
  Faces in the crowd : reaching your international neighbor for Christ /
by Donna S. Thomas.
    p. cm.
  ISBN 978-1-59669-205-3 (sc)
  1. Church work with immigrants--United States. 2. Evangelistic
work--United States. I. Title.
  BV639.I4T56 2008
  248.'5--dc22
                            2008020400

Cover Design by Gearbox; www.studiogearbox.com
Interior Design by Sherry Hunt

ISBN-10: 1-59669-205-7
ISBN-13: 978-1-59669-205-3

N084131 0908 4M1

With love and appreciation to

Claude and Jan Robold—

my cheerleaders and my friends

Contents

Foreword

Not long ago three different cultures met head-on at my lunch table. At a Mexican restaurant in central Indiana, the chips and salsa arrived in the hands of a young man from Eastern Europe. Between refills of diet cola we sustained something of a running conversation.

"What work do you do?" he asked.

When I explained that I help lead a group of people who endeavor to follow the teachings of Jesus, he immediately replied, "I'm trying to learn more about that."

We traded phone numbers and promised to keep in touch. It occurred to me that I knew someone in our church who would be excited to hear about my lunchtime experience: Donna Thomas.

Little did I know that Donna was one step ahead of me. She had already eaten a burrito at that restaurant, entered into conversation with the same young man, spoken quietly about the adventure of pursuing Jesus, and invited him to worship. I don't know anyone who has a passion for international ministry here in the United States quite like Donna Thomas.

Visit the restaurants, businesses, and campuses of almost any US community and you'll find men and women who didn't attend the local high school. They grew up halfway around the world. It's entirely possible that the number of internationals—visiting workers and students as well as recent immigrants—in your community has doubled since the beginning of this century (2000).

While the world may have moved in just down your street, you may not be blessed to live near someone like Donna, who is uniquely called and gifted to model a new kind of missions work. This book is your chance to learn from a special teacher. As her pastor I have been moved by the vision she imparts and have seen it shift both our congregation and our community. Through these pages, you too will encounter her wisdom, her experience, and her relentless eagerness to share God's good news through newfound friendships.

Consider this book a missiological companion to Thomas L. Friedman's best seller, *The World Is Flat.* Friedman demonstrates how the barriers of time and space that used to separate the world's continents have functionally disappeared. A growing proportion of the world's population has access to powerful economic and educational opportunities. Entrepreneurs are linking nation to nation through creative new partnerships.

Spiritual entrepreneurs have seized the moment as well. The "flattening" of God's world brings all of us, right here and right now, into contact with those whose names and faces, in previous generations, would have forever remained unknown. Now they are our neighbors. And our coworkers. And the servers at our lunch table tomorrow. Ours is an unprecedented opportunity to fulfill Jesus's Great Commission of making disciples of all nations. The nations have quite literally come to us.

Let Donna help show the way. Get ready for an adventure. Get ready to meet the world...right next door.

Reverend Glenn McDonald
Senior Pastor
Zionsville Presbyterian Church
Zionsville, Indiana

Acknowledgments

What a treasure God has given me in my friend and editor, Karen Roberts. Without her, this book would not be in your hands. Her fingers are on every page, and her encouragement has brought it to completion.

Dozens of my friends shared their lives and stories and gave me permission to share them with you. The stories are true, but in some cases, I have changed names and places to protect confidentiality. These are precious friends with a generous spirit.

Louie Moesta, Bob and Peggy Lazard, and Val Angove took pen in hand to proofread the final manuscript. I am continually appreciative of the support and encouragement of Holly Miller. She is a number one cheerleader. I am thankful for the contributions of each of these individuals.

I am deeply grateful for my family, who support my efforts, for my agent, Les Stobbe, who encourages me, and for Church at the Crossing and Zionsville Presbyterian, who endorse my ministry.

The one who asked me to write this book and share it with you is none other than my Lord and Master, Jesus Christ. He teaches me how to do what I write about, He gives me joy as I follow His direction and plant His seeds, and He is the one that makes the seeds grow. Without Him, I am nothing and I can do nothing. My question to Him each morning is "OK, Lord, what do you have in store for me today?" I want to serve Him and be His bond slave all the days of my life.

Introduction

Living the Adventure

A few months ago, I decided to try out a new restaurant. As I was a bit early that evening, few people were there yet. The booth I was led to was in the back, directly in front of a huge painting of an ancient scene covering the entire wall. A young man was prompt with the restaurant's special hot bread and his question about what I would like to drink.

When he returned with my cola, I asked, "How do you like working here? Is this a pretty good place to work?" He was easy to talk with.

When he brought my dinner, I discovered that his name was Eugen and that he was from Bulgaria. He had been in this country for a few years, and he wanted to become a doctor. Since I like to talk with people, and servers are usually interesting, I enjoyed our conversation.

It was such an enjoyable experience that I went back a week later and asked to be seated in Eugen's area again. He seemed glad to see me when I remembered his name. Our conversation picked up between that special bread, the dinner, and the refills of my cola. It was his turn for questions.

"Where do you work?" he asked.

I love that question. I could answer, "I'm retired," which would be true, but that usually ends a conversation. Or I could say, "I'm a grandma and just enjoy being with my grandchildren." Another end to conversation. Instead, I choose to say, "I have this strange notion that I'm to write another book, so I've been working on that."

Of course he wanted to know what it was about, and about my other books too. "What kind of books are they?" he asked. "I read a lot, but I've never considered writing a book."

I told him they were Christian books. About that time, he was called away by another customer. I finished my dinner, paid my bill, and left.

A week or so later, I went to that restaurant again and asked to sit in his area. The huge smile on his face told me that he remembered me. It wasn't long into the typical small talk that he said, "Would it be possible for me to have one of your books? How could I get one? I would like to read it."

Just ask me that and watch out—you might have a book in your hand. I told him I had one with me. After I finished my meal and paid my bill, I went to the trunk of my car, pulled out *Climb Another Mountain,* the story of my spiritual journey, and took it in to him.

I went to the restaurant again a couple weeks later, that time with a growing awareness that God was doing something in the life of this young man. I wanted to do everything I could to be available to help.

While he was setting the special bread and a cola on my table, he said, "I read your book. It is really interesting. I like your stories. Where do you go to church?"

That was an easy question to answer. His next question was, "Could I go with you sometime?" That was easy to answer too.

"Of course you can go with me. When would you like to go?"

We made plans for me to pick him up the next Sunday, and we continued our conversation between his taking care of other customers and having time to stop by my table.

Those visits to that restaurant were the beginning in developing a life-changing relationship with this young man from Bulgaria. I detected that he was lonesome. He told me that he didn't really know anything about church or religion. I introduced him to a class of people at my church who were about his age. After that first Sunday, I invited him to come on his own. Every Sunday I looked for him to come. He showed up sometimes for church, and sometimes he didn't make it.

Each time I went to that restaurant, Eugen and I continued to develop our friendship. He asked me questions about right and wrong, about Christianity, and about the Bible. The day came when I felt it was right to give him a Bible. *Good News for Modern Man* seemed just the perfect one, as it is easy to read and understand, especially for a beginner.

"Eugen," I said, "the Bible is divided into two sections, the Old Testament and the New Testament. Start reading in the New Testament on page 41, the part called 'The Gospel of Mark.' Write down any questions you have, and we'll talk about them."

Several visits to the restaurant later, he said, "Could you take me to church this Sunday? My car is broken down and is being fixed, but it won't be available Sunday. May I go with you?"

"I'll be happy to pick you up, Eugen. Be ready at eight o'clock, and we'll be on our way."

Because of our many conversations, him telling me that he was reading the Bible, and his questions about spiritual things, I felt it was time to talk to him about a commitment to the Lord. That Sunday morning, I was praying, "OK, Lord, I'll take him to church, but afterwards I want to take him to a coffee shop and present the plan of salvation to him. Let me know if this is what I should do."

Sunday morning came, and he was waiting. The greeter at church was his usual friendly self. The ushers knew where I always sit, and we made our way down the aisle toward the front. Good sermon, great singing, and wonderful atmosphere. We prayed the benediction and took our place near the end of the line to shake the pastor's hand.

"Donna, I have some interesting news to tell you about my trip last week in Michigan," the pastor said as we shook hands. "Wait on me, will you?"

Eugen and I stepped to the side. When the pastor was finally free, he came to us and moved us next to the wall in the lobby, since he felt he would not be interrupted there. He told Eugen and me his news. Suddenly God impressed on me that this was the time. I turned to Eugen and said, "Eugen, are you ready to give your heart to God and be His child?"

"Uhh, no. Uhh, yes," he stuttered. He was ready, and this was the time and the place.

I asked some more questions to enable him to affirm that he did indeed want to be a child of God. Then the pastor asked him to repeat after him the prayer of a sinner repenting and asking to be forgiven and to be God's child. As we lifted our heads after the prayer, happiness, joy, and peace shone on our faces.

Eugen is now one of God's children, and it happened right there in the church lobby, up against one of the walls, with people coming and going all around us who had no clue that the Lord was bringing another soul into His kingdom right in front of them.

Of course, I went back to that restaurant a few days later. "I sure feel good now," Eugen told me in the middle of our conversation.

Another waiter stopped to talk with us. I introduced myself and found out his name was Rin. It was a wonderful surprise when he asked me, "Do you go to church with Eugen?"

It was easy simply to say, "Yes, I do."

Rin went on to ask me if he could come to church with us too. When I left the restaurant, I was almost jumping for joy, reliving how I could see God working and that I was a part of it. I began praying for Rin and asking the Lord to bring him into the kingdom too.

The next time I was enjoying talking with Eugen and Rin and eating that bread, another server came over. This beautiful young lady looked like she might be from India.

"Are you Eugen's grandmother?" she asked.

"Well, yes, I am now. I just became his grandmother a few weeks ago."

"He was telling me about you, and I wanted to meet you."

"Great. Now tell me your name."

"I'm Usam."

"Where are you from, Usam?"

"From Pakistan, but I've lived here quite a while."

"So what do you do when you're not working here?"

"I'm studying at the university. I want to be a doctor too like Eugen."

Eugen came back to my table, so our conversation ended and she left.

The story of Eugen coming to know Christ as his Savior because of a few visits to a restaurant and some God-directed conversation is just one example of the adventure the Lord has for all of us as His twenty-first century disciples. Obviously, there is no end to this story. Meeting Eugen first, then Rin, and then Usam shows me that the Lord is in it. It is only the beginning.

My great desire is that these pages will give you the challenge and the tools to find your Eugen and many others and to lead them to the Lord. This book is written especially to help you do that. We collaborate with God. He bestows the gift of amazing grace on undeserving and unsuspecting people like you and like me.

Chapter 1

Anywhere Will Do

"For I know the plans I have for you."
—Jeremiah 29:11

As I walked into the coffee shop, the warm aroma of brewing coffee stimulated my taste buds. Yes, this was where I wanted to be. Picking up my latte and scone, I looked around for someone who looked in need of a friend.

Off in one corner, I saw a younger woman who I thought just might be from another country, maybe India. Since she was alone, I wondered if we could get acquainted and enjoy this time together. Maybe she was the one the Lord wanted me to talk with this morning.

Her gaze was toward the window, but as I approached, she looked my way.

"Is anyone joining you?" I asked.

"No," she replied and extended a gesture of welcome toward the other chair.

"Thank you." I settled across from her and mentally pulled out an opening conversation starter. "Do you come here often?" I asked.

She smiled. "Quite a bit, but not every day. How about you?"

"I haven't been to this coffee shop before, but I do search for a good and tasty cup from time to time. Tell me, are you from around here or somewhere else?"

Her eyes lit up as she realized I really wanted to know about her. She had apparently discovered that many people in the United States are too busy and too preoccupied to notice her or even look her way.

"Actually, I'm from India," she said, watching me to see my reaction.

"Oh my! So far away. What city in India? How long have you been here?"

"I'm from Mumbai, but most people know it as Bombay. The government changed the name back to its original one a few years ago. I've been here nine months now." A smile crept across her face as she answered me.

"Really. You certainly have experienced a lot of cultural differences, haven't you? Do you work around here?" I asked, returning her smile.

"Yes, this country is so very different than mine, and I have so much to learn about it. And yes, I work just down the street in that office building. Fortunately, I earned a degree in computer science in Mumbai, and it seems American companies are hiring a lot of us. My job is interesting, and it pays well. Most importantly, I can have a future here that is not available to me at home."

Her smile was telling me as much as her words. She seemed to enjoy the opportunity to talk one-on-one with an American who was interested in her.

"Oh, by the way, my name is Donna. What is yours?" I finally asked.

"Bina."

"Bina. That's a pretty name. Tell me about Mumbai and what it was like growing up there."

Getting to Know Bina

As Bina set her cup of coffee aside, I could tell she was enjoying talking to me about her life back home. Her eyes were bright. Her face was shining. She told me about her family and what life was like in Mumbai. Since I had been there, I knew enough about India and Mumbai to ask some engaging questions.

When she paused once, I asked. "Bina, I know India is a Hindu country basically, but there are lots of Muslims, Buddhists, Jains, and Christians there too. What is your religion?"

"I'm a Hindu. All my relatives are Hindu. What about you? Are you a...a Christian?"

"Yes, Bina, I'm a Christian, and that is a choice here in America. Not all Americans are Christians. Here we have the freedom to choose our religion. You will find Americans who are Christians and many Americans who are not."

"Oh, really? So you chose to become a Christian?"

"Yes, I did." I was remembering that time and praying for the best way to tell this young woman from India about it.

"I chose to become a Christian several years ago. I didn't like my life, and I just knew in my heart that there must be something more. I went to a church meeting and heard about Jesus. Now that is quite a story, but here is the shortened version. The leader, we call him a pastor, was talking about sin and displeasing God. I knew I had sinned, and it felt awful. As he continued, he told the people there how to get rid of that sin. He said we only have to repent for what we have done, ask God for forgiveness, and start living to please him."

"I've never heard of that."

"Well, Bina, the pastor was using a book called the Holy Bible that gives all of this information. I had a Bible and had read some of it, but I needed someone to tell me exactly how it all worked. That day, the day I repented of my sins and accepted the forgiveness of God, is the day I became a Christian. It was really quite simple when I made the decision to try living God's way."

"Then, Donna, do you like being a Christian? Does it help you? I guess I really want to ask, how does it help you?"

I whispered a quick prayer and answered. "Bina, it is a precious and wonderful experience. God helped me that very day by forgiving my sins. He gave me peace and the unique privilege of being His child. Imagine that, Bina. I'm a child of God. And now, God—we Christians call Him the Lord—helps me each day by being with me in spirit and helping me with my choices. The Bible helps me as I read it too, because it tells me how the Lord wants me to live. And best of all, I have peace and joy."

I looked into her eyes to see if she seemed OK with my answer. She did, so I continued.

"I discovered that, once you're a Christian, there are basically two rules to follow. Not bad, huh? The first one is to love the Lord your God with all your heart, all your soul, and all your might. The second rule is to love your neighbor, or other people, as you do yourself."

"Just two rules? That's not many," Bina responded.

"Yes, Bina, just two. As we obey these two rules, we keep that special peace with God and enjoy the wonderful privilege of being His child. Besides that, other people can tell who we Christians are by our actions and love for each other. Jesus told us this truth when He was here on earth. He said that love, concern, and service to others are the attributes of Christians. He also showed us what He meant by His actions. Have you heard of Jesus?"

"Well I've heard that name, but I don't really know anything about Him." Glancing at her watch, she continued, "I really do want to know, but I am running out of time. Maybe we can meet here again. Will that work?" She pushed back her chair.

"Sure, Bina. Would you want to meet tomorrow, same

time? I would be delighted to have coffee with you again and talk further."

As she gathered her things to go, she said, "Yes. This has been wonderful. Thank you for coming over to sit with me. I will be waiting for you here in the morning."

"Great," I said. "Here's my phone number if you need to call me. I'll see you tomorrow."

The Rest of the Story

You can be sure that I spent some time in prayer that night for Bina. I did want her to be waiting for me in the morning. I certainly wanted to continue our conversation about Jesus. I prayed she would come with questions and an earnest desire to learn about Jesus. As I entered the coffee shop the next morning, I was still praying that she would be there, and she was.

"Hi, Bina. Great to see you. Let me get my latte, and I'll be right there."

The big smile on her face let me know she was as eager to continue our relationship as I was. After coming back to her table and exchanging the usual greetings and chitchat, I steered the conversation toward Jesus.

"Bina, you said yesterday that you had heard of Jesus but you didn't know anything about Him. I can tell you about Him, but I really have to start at the beginning, which is about the Creator, God Almighty. Do you really want me to tell you about God and Jesus?"

"Of course. I want to know about Jesus and your God and what a Christian is, so please do tell me."

"OK. Yesterday I mentioned the Holy Bible. It is a book of sacred writings. It says that God made the world in the beginning. God made the land, the oceans, the trees, the animals, and all that is in this world. Then God decided He would like to make people so He could have companionship with them. That is when He made a man, and named him Adam, and a woman, and named her Eve."

Bina interrupted, "Is that really how the world was started? I haven't heard any of this story before."

"Yes, Bina." I caught my breath and went on.

"God was enjoying the companionship of Adam and Eve, but since He wanted them to enjoy being with Him by their own choice, He gave them an option. They could listen to Him and enjoy His companionship, or they could decide to do things He had already told them were wrong. He called those things sin. Sure enough, there came a time when Adam and Eve chose sin and turned their backs on God."

She was listening intently, so I continued. "Their sin caused God great distress. He wanted to resume His special relationship with them and with their children. After many years, God began selecting people to be His prophets so they could tell everybody about Him. Some people listened to those prophets and straightened up, but many didn't. Those who listened and worshiped God as Creator, He blessed. Those who continued to sin, hurt Him so much that He could not have companionship with them."

"OK, Donna, but just where does Jesus fit into all of this? I want to know about Him too," Bina interjected.

"Bina, Jesus came into this story at just the right time, but it wasn't yet. You see, God continued sending prophets or messengers to tell people about Him for hundreds of years. It was because of God's great love for people that He continued sending prophets, wanting as many people as possible to believe in Him. Finally, the time was just right, so God sent His Son into the world. He sent Jesus. God sent Him to the earth so He could tell everyone directly about God and bring anyone who would listen into that companionship God wanted. This truth is recorded in the Holy Bible where it says, 'God so loved the world that He gave His one and only Son, that whoever believes in Him shall not perish but have eternal life' (John 3:16). His Son, Jesus, lived in Israel at the time the Roman Empire controlled Jerusalem."

I was amazed at how intently Bina was listening. It was time to bring the conversation back around to her.

"Jesus's whole message was to show us how to have a precious and wonderful relationship with God and live a life pleasing to Him. Now, Bina, what do you think of God and Jesus? Have you ever heard anything like this before?"

"No, Donna, I haven't. What an amazing story. Is it really true? Did all of those things really happen?"

"Yes, they did. Everything in this story really happened. There's a lot more to the story, and I do want to share it with you. The most important part is that Jesus is alive in heaven today. As we Christians pray to Him and ask Him to help us, we enjoy a precious relationship with Him and with God, His Father."

She looked a little confused but still open.

"What I'm really saying is this. God so loved you, Bina, that He sent His one and only Son, Jesus, so that when you believe in Him, you will have a new life—an eternal life. If you choose to believe in Jesus and accept what He says, God will put you in His family and you will have a personal and unique relationship with Him. Just think of that, Bina. God has a family of people here on earth, and He wants you and me to be in it. In God's family, God becomes your heavenly Father, and you have His special love and concern for you."

Bina was wide-eyed. She had never in her whole life heard anything like what I was telling her.

"Bina, I brought some of the Holy Bible for you. It's called the New Testament, and it tells about Jesus. You may take it home with you. Here," I said as I turned to the Book of John. "Here is a part I am sure you will want to read. As you read it, write down any questions that come to your mind, and the next time we get together, we can discuss them. OK?"

A Friendship Started

This coffee shop conversation was the beginning of my friendship with Bina. It started simply. It developed as we continued to meet and I was there to answer her questions. What an exciting adventure. It was simply a matter of seeing her, starting a conversation, developing a relationship, and sharing what Christ means to me. Yes, it took time. But it was precious time.

Several months after our first encounter in that coffee shop, this lonesome woman from Mumbai, India, had the opportunity to ask Jesus to come into her heart. She chose to follow Him and become a child of God. I can only imagine how many friends here in the US and also back in India she will tell about Jesus and how she first heard of Him.

In previous years, we American Christians had to go thousands of miles to share the gospel with the people of India. Today the people of India and nearly every other nation on the earth are coming to us. They are often in the coffee shops and the fast-food restaurants, and some are working in our stores. As you see them and realize that they have come from another part of the world, check what God is doing in your heart. Opportunities are all around you. You only have to look first and then use the words the Lord gives you to make a connection.

What About You?

How often do you come across people from another country? Would you like to meet a Bina or perhaps a Samish, Juan, or Lidia? Yes, you would like the Lord to use you to share what it means to be a Christian with them, but do you know how? Are you afraid because you don't know how to start? What if redirecting a person's eternity really was as simple as seeing that person and starting a conversation?

I imagine you have some divine discontent in your soul right now, a bit of yearning to be Jesus's messenger today. Maybe you never thought about becoming a missionary.

That's OK. *As a Christian you already are one.*

I pray this book will help you enjoy sharing Christ with people from other countries and experience the blessings it brings. It is not a difficult task. Your smallest effort turns into a great blessing for you and life-saving news to those the Lord puts in your path.

Have you ever wanted to lift weights, run marathons, do the impossible, and be a winner? This book will show you the way to become a twenty-first-century disciple, a winner with the Lord. And yes, that means becoming a *world changer*.

The Lord's Great Commission is not a suggestion. It is a command—for His disciples. Who are His disciples today? You are. I am. All of us who claim Jesus as Lord are His disciples. The Great Commission is for all of us, all of His disciples. It is His plan for making our lives count. Read on, and you'll find the path to follow.

Something to Consider

Can you picture yourself doing what I did with Bina?
Pray about it.
Read about the Samaritan woman in John 4:4–38. Are there any parallels in the story of the Samaritan woman and the story of Bina? What do you see?

_____

_____

_____

_____

_____

_____

Action Steps

What will it take to get you ready to meet your Bina?
Write down how you feel.
Date what you wrote and put it in your Bible.
Share it with a trusted friend this week.

Write and memorize the Great Commission that Jesus gave
in Matthew 28:19–20. _____

_____

_____

_____

_____

_____

_____

_____

Chapter 2

Strangers Among Us

Commit to the LORD whatever you do, and your plans will succeed.
—Proverbs 16:3

I have a habit of counting things. I count steps and traffic lights. I also count people who might be from another country. I'm up to five today, and it's only 2 P.M.

At the post office this morning, I heard a mom whispering in another language to her baby. That was two. After a stop at the local video shop, I added two more who were employees with foreign accents. When I ordered my hamburger, it seemed obvious to me that the clerk was from somewhere other than this country. That made five.

Muslim women are easy to spot if they are wearing a head covering, and I'm beginning to recognize men from the Middle East as well. Those brick masons working down the street speak Spanish. I wonder where they are from. The lady who sat beside me at the concert the other night is from Argentina. I know because I asked her.

At a local strip mall near my home outside Indianapolis, I did an informal survey, and of 301 employees in 35 shops, 74 are immigrants. They come from 12 different countries.

Where have I been? It seems like so many people who look and speak differently than me have arrived recently. I wonder why they are here.

Are you discovering them around you too? Think about it. How many people of different appearance or dress do you think you encounter when you are out and about shopping during any given week? Where do you think they come from?

I guess it is time for me to open my eyes and my heart and realize that God has me, you, and them here for His purpose.

Looking Around

I haven't always seen strangers through God's eyes. No, the Lord started working on me several years ago when my late husband, Chuck, and I, along with our three boys, made our first trip to Mexico. We didn't know anything about Mexicans. We couldn't speak their language. But we'd been challenged by an evangelist, Larry DeShay, who visited the church where my husband was serving as pastor. He told my husband, "You're never going to be doing all you can for the Lord unless you get a heart for missions.

At the time, we were basically saying to ourselves, *Why should we? We have enough to do at the church as it is.* But we accepted that challenge, and it turned into a great blessing that totally changed our lives.

From my vantage point, with all those years behind me, I can see how the Lord had His plans all along. If He had told me then all that I would be doing and what He had in mind for me, I would have run like Jonah and said, "I won't." I would have used Moses's response and said, "I can't. No, not me, Lord. Choose someone else. I can't do anything like that." I could have even chosen Isaiah's response and said, "I'm not good enough" and the Apostle Peter's fearful response, "I'm afraid."

That first trip to Mexico in 1962, driving more than 1,000 miles from Wichita, Kansas, to Saltillo in our blue station wagon, was the initial step the Lord had for my husband and me. And the Lord didn't stop with it. He continued to give us more challenges, more steps in obedience to Him.

Not "Why?" but "Why Not?"

After we returned home from Saltillo, the Lord asked us to buy a road bus and start taking other people south to Mexico. "Why should we do that Lord? Oh, OK." It worked. Our church, like us, learned to see the world differently.

About four years later, the Lord whispered in our ears, "There is more than Mexico. Get a big airplane and take people all over the Caribbean and Latin America." That was when God was teaching us to say, "Why not?" instead of, "Why?"

We found a 40-passenger plane, raised the money, and bought it. At the same time, Chuck, who had had his pilot's license for almost 15 years at the time, had to go through the time-consuming and expensive process of getting type rated to fly a plane that big. Can you imagine what people were saying to us then? Oh, some were encouraging us, while others told us we must be crazy. But the Lord helped us each step of the way. And what adventures we had.

Short-term missions were unheard of at that time, but after we realized how we could help a pastor in Guatemala, we started taking teams to build church buildings wherever we discovered the need. Soon Nicaragua had a massive earthquake. Our hearts told us we had to respond. Teams were recruited and supplies were located as we led trip after trip, responding to the devastated people in Managua.

"Now do we get to quit, Lord?" Of course not. We were just starting. And we didn't want to quit anyway. We were soon taking thousands of volunteers to build churches, clinics, and schools in country after country.

Did we encounter problems? Certainly. Bureaucracies and red tape are in every country. We faced the need of dollars to do the jobs, the various language difficulties, the cultural challenges, plus the growing desire to do more.

Yes, the Lord opened our eyes to the people of the world in Mexico, and then He continued in Central America and the Caribbean. It wasn't long before we were urged to help in South America. At that time, we thought the Western Hemisphere would be as far as we would go, but the Lord had more in His plans for us.

Over the following years, Project Partner, the missions ministry my husband and I founded, expanded worldwide as we helped Christians in many countries with construction, medical ministry, pastoral training, and more. The national Christian leaders we've assisted have seen their own ministries blossom, resulting in countless new believers. Chuck went to be with the Lord in 1992. I stepped away from Project Partner in 1999. I didn't retire though; I changed careers. I founded a writing, speaking, and consulting ministry, Christian Vision Ministries, to continue to help take the gospel to the world. And yes, this gives me a healthy travel and speaking schedule.

Here I am counting again, and as I count them up, I find that the Lord has had me involved in 79 countries thus far, some of them many times. Here is why I enjoy counting. It shows me the wonderful opportunities the Lord gives me wherever I may be. It causes me to celebrate.

Now I can easily spot someone from India, China, or other countries I've visited. When I start a conversation with them, they are excited that I know about their country and equally excited that I am giving them my attention.

I had lunch the other day at a Thai restaurant. It was a blessing to me to be able to talk with the people who work there about their homeland. I plan to go back and continue our conversation. As I was writing this chapter, I heard from my Saudi Arabian friend, whom I met here in the States. He sent me an update on what is going on in his life. Today my email brought me a message from my friend who is back in

Sierra Leone and another one from a young man I met here who is on his way to Jordan.

I consider it a great privilege to plant the seed of the gospel. Sometimes I can watch it grow. Sometimes I can harvest. Many more times than these, however, I have to trust the Lord to send someone else to water the seed and bring it to maturity. It is a joy and privilege to be His disciple.

Yes, I like to count, but it is up to the Lord to make the final count. I trust Him to produce the results. Though I will never know how some of my encounters with strangers turn out, it's OK. I just want to do my part, to be obedient, to respond to the nudging from the Lord.

Internationals Everywhere

I live in a community that prints its own neighborhood directory every year. As I look at the names in it, I see some names that are strange to me. For instance, I see Tamhankar, Choe, Li, Raghuraman, Sufipto, Lin Yu-Huan, Kachhwaha, Chiu, Cavagnini, Weng, Zelikovich, and Zhao. Not the typical American names that I am used to like Jones, Smith, Brown, and even Thomas.

Maybe some of these people have been in Indiana a long time. But many have probably moved here recently. Why do they choose to move thousands of miles from family and home? I am trying to answer this question.

As I get to know them, they all seem to be looking for a future and the resources to provide for their family, not unlike any of us. However, I cannot imagine leaving my comfort zone to live in a country I don't know, with people whose language I do not speak, who have a culture I don't understand—so far away from family and friends.

They tell me that basically they are here because of opportunities—opportunities for a job, a career, a future, a way to help those they left behind financially. Sometimes they've come for freedom to live the life they want. Several of them have jobs in the computer field. A couple of them are working in different aspects of medicine. One is the owner of a successful Indian restaurant.

I am reminded of the story in the New Testament about Philip, one of Jesus's disciples (Acts 8:26–40). Jesus had told all of His followers to go make disciples. Following God's direction, Philip was simply walking down the road from his home (Jerusalem) one day when he came across a foreigner, an Ethiopian. The Ethiopian had apparently been in Jerusalem looking for some answers for his life. Philip encountered him, and he had the opportunity to tell him about Jesus.

As you read the story, you can see how Philip led the Ethiopian to belief in Christ in his initial encounter. He was ready. The Ethiopian just needed someone to explain the gospel to him.

It doesn't look like Philip planned any of what happened that day. He was just at the right place at the right time and was available to be used by God.

My friend Eldon had much the same encounter. Well, not exactly. He went to a fast-food restaurant and encountered the manager, Mathew. Later he was able to talk with Mathew about the Lord and answer his questions. This story is still in progress. Mathew wants to know more, and Eldon is being used by God to be the messenger.

Most of our encounters are not like Philip's, with immediate results, or even like Eldon's. And they don't have to be. We are working at being faithful to the Lord, not racking up points as to whom and how many we lead to Christ.

Last month I had an encounter similar to Eldon's. I met a man from western Africa behind the counter at a fast-food restaurant. As he was taking my order, I asked him where he was from and why he was here. The first encounter opened the door for me to talk with him again. After several times talking with him, I invited him and his family to my house for supper.

He came with his wife and a friend named Fayez. Before we sat down to dinner, they looked around my house at my artifacts. They could see that I had been to several countries. They asked me questions about my life, what I do, where I have been, and what I have encountered. I saw that this evening was my chance to tell them how the Lord has directed my life. Over dinner, I answered their questions, sharing some of my story.

I could have told them about the good times and the blessings I've received from my Lord. I chose to tell them instead about difficult and hard times and how the Lord held my hand and took me through them. They wanted to know about dangerous times in some of my travels. I had those stories too. After a few stories, I was able to tell them how the Lord is my "Abba Father," how He made me His child when I asked Him to, and about the love that He has for me.

They asked me just the questions I love to answer. It was a wonderful evening focusing on the Lord. The best part was that they were asking me the questions, and my part was simply to answer them.

As our conversation continued, I was thinking, *How did I get myself into this anyway?* This in itself is a miracle, considering how shy I used to be.

That evening the seed of the gospel was planted. No conversion yet, as they are still processing our conversation, but you can be sure I am praying for them and will plan another time together.

You don't have to go to Mexico. You don't have to go to Judea to be a twenty-first-century disciple of Jesus. You don't even have to go overseas. Just look around you. The world has come to you in Anytown, USA. Hispanics, Asians, Africans, people from China and India, and many others are right in front of you everywhere you go. These and people of many more nationalities have moved to America and live here, some right in your neighborhood.

Look at the clerk in the department store, the waiter at the restaurant, the owner of the specialty shop, the teller at the bank. You'll soon realize, as I have, that you don't have to go 8,000 miles to be a missionary. The distance could be little more than 24 inches, the distance between your face and the face of a new friend.

Christian America?

Just because people who appear to be of a different nationality have moved down the street from you, here in the heart of "Christian America," they don't necessarily know what you know about our Lord. In fact, even if they think they know about Christians, you can be sure they have some strange misconceptions. Consider this.

Right after 9/11, I felt I needed to relate with some Muslims. I didn't know any and didn't know where to start. A friend told me to call the local university. I took a deep breath, looked up the phone number, dialed it, and asked if the university had any international students. The receptionist connected me to the international student director.

My next question was, "Do you have any students from the Middle East who would like some help with their English?" The director gave me a phone number and the name "Manzur." OK, with that name, it looked like I was going in the right direction.

I called Manzur, and we set up a time to meet at a coffee shop on campus. That was easy. He was a good-looking young man from Saudi Arabia in his junior year. We talked that day about his family and my family, and our friendship was off to a good start. At our next session, he answered my questions about Islam. The third session, I answered his about Christianity. He asked some amazing questions.

"Donna," he said, "I have been told that all Americans are Christians."

I just about dropped my cup of coffee when he said that. How strange that anyone could think everybody in America is a Christian.

"Manzur," I responded, "that is not true. Where did you hear that?"

"Well, that is what I have always been told. Back home in Saudi Arabia, we are told that everybody here is a Christian—all the TV programs are Christian, and all the movies are Christian. For this reason, I am very cautious as to whom I choose as friends."

I was so glad he had asked me that question. He had been here in the United States for two years, all the while believing a lie about Christianity. I caught my breath, praying for the Lord's help in answering him.

"Manzur, America was founded on Christian principles by mostly Christian people, but this is a country of freedom. Our government does not control our religion. Everyone has the option of choosing a religion here. Some Americans are Christians and some are not, but certainly not all Americans are Christians. Unfortunately, there are lots of Americans who aren't Christians. You can't put all Americans in the same category."

"I didn't know that," he replied. "Some of the things I see and hear don't sound right, and I don't like a lot of what I see Americans doing. But if not everybody is a Christian, how can I know who is and who isn't?"

"Good question, Manzur. You can't tell Christians by what they wear. You can't tell Christians by any mark on their forehead. Here is how to tell who is a Christian, and this answer is actually in the Holy Bible. Jesus says that you can tell Christians by their actions and their love. He tells us to love the Lord our God and to love our neighbor as ourselves. As we do this, you can tell who is a Christian."

"Oh, OK. That sounds better," Manzur responded, "because I don't approve of some things I see students doing and some things I see on TV and in some movies.

Hmm. Your answer does change the picture for me of who Christians are."

Your Neighborhood

Before those from other countries came to live in your city, town, or neighborhood, they probably heard, like Manzur did, that America is a Christian country. They probably believed that all Americans are Christians. How wrong they were! One look at a newspaper surely must have confused them about Christian behavior. If they think what they see advertised in the newspapers, on suggestive covers of magazines, in the movies, and on television is "Christian," would they ever want to be a Christian? Certainly not a high-caste Brahmin. Definitely not a Muslim.

Who is going to tell them the true story, as I was able to tell Manzur? They need someone to break down their misconceptions. Could you be the one?

According to *The World Almanac and Book of Facts 2007*, there are 5.7 million Jews, 4.6 million Muslims, 2.7 million Buddhists, and 1.1 million Hindus living in the United States. Add the Sikhs, Baha'i, tribal religionists, the nonreligious, and others who are not Christians to that figure, and you know that disciples in the twenty-first century have a big job to do. Jesus told His first-century disciples to go to Jerusalem, Judea, Samaria, and to the ends of the earth and preach the gospel. In our century, Jerusalem, Judea, Samaria, and the rest of the world have come to us.

When I think about William Carey, the first missionary to India, and what he had to do to reach the unreached people there, I sure am glad our world is different. Carey arrived in India in 1793 as a missionary-reformer, the first modern Protestant emissary from the English-speaking world to the non-English speaking world. Missionaries at that time said good-bye to families and friends and boarded a ship, never expecting to come home again. Communication with home? Seldom, and, if possible by letter, it took months to get there.

Phones? Not invented yet. Food? Totally different. A house? Sort of, but nothing like what was left behind. Medical care? Unheard of. Times have changed—and so has our world.

One thing has not changed, however. Millions of people still do not know about Jesus, and thousands more are being born every day. Despite strategic efforts by modern missionaries and evangelists, the evangelism explosion of the twentieth century just could not keep up with the population explosion. And now, in the global society of our twenty-first century, the unreached people of the world are all around us.

Luckily for us, it's easier in many ways to be obedient to Jesus's command than it was back then. All we have to do is see the people from other countries right here among us, make friends with them, build a relationship, and at the right time, tell them what Jesus Christ means to us.

Something to Consider

Can you picture yourself talking to a Muslim or a Hindu? Pray about it.

Write down how you feel. _____

_____

_____

_____

_____

_____

_____

_____

Action Steps

Ask the Lord to help you see these internationals and know how to reach them.

Start a conversation with someone you know or think is from a different country. Ask where your new acquaintance is from. Learn about his or her country. Ask about his or her religion.

Look in your local phone book and see what churches for ethnic groups are in your city. List those ethnic churches here.

_____

_____

_____

_____

_____

_____

_____

_____

_____

_____

_____

Something More to Consider

Globalization?

This is it, my friend.

We hear a lot about globalization these days...an example follows.

Question: What is the height of globalization?

Answer: Princess Diana's death.

Question: How come?

Answer: An English princess with an Egyptian boyfriend crashes in a French tunnel, driving a German car with a Dutch engine, driven by a Belgian who was high on Scottish whiskey, followed closely by Italian Paparazzi, on Japanese motorcycles, treated by an American doctor, using Brazilian medicines!

And this is sent to you by an Indian, using Bill Gates technology, which he took from the Japanese. And you may be reading this on one of the IBM clones using Taiwanese-made chips, and Korean-made monitors, assembled by Bangladeshi workers in a Singapore plant, transported by lorries driven by Pakistanis, hijacked by Indonesians, and finally sold to you by Chinese!

This widely distributed Internet joke makes a point, doesn't it?

Here are some more serious examples of how the world is shrinking from the Lausanne Committee for World Evangelization.

http://www.lausanne.org/documents/2004forum/LOP30_IG1.pdf

- A man in London calls a product help-line for his IBM computer and gets an operator in Bangalore.

- A German protestor in Berlin organizes an anti-globalization demonstration in Brazil with fellow organizers in Taipei, Mexico City, and Seattle, via email.

- Filipina maids in Riyadh, Saudi Arabia see themselves as missionaries to their wealthy Arab Muslim employers.

- A Japanese pilot communicates in English to the Thai air-traffic controllers upon approach to Bangkok.

- Rural Nigerians come to faith in Christ by watching The Jesus Film. (Global missions organizations have translated the film into 830 languages.)

- A Chinese college student passes the SARS virus to a relative visiting from Hong Kong, who in turn passes it to a friend from Canada. Within a few days, a SARS outbreak occurs in Toronto.

- Researchers at the Carter Center in Atlanta, Georgia, discover a cure for River Blindness in Africa.

- Nuclear waste is taken from Japan and reprocessed in Sellafield, England, before being dumped in Australia.

Chapter 3

Where Is the World?

Go!
Go where?
Around the block,
 down the street,
 across town—
 find the world!

Have you heard of the 10/40 window? Probably not, because it's a region of the world that is not known as a tourist spot. It is the area from 10 degrees to 40 degrees north of the equator, extending from the edge of the Atlantic Ocean across North Africa and the Middle East all the way to the far side of Asia. It is a term coined in 1990 by missiologist Luis Bush to highlight this large area with urgent physical and spiritual needs.

Most of the people in the world who have never heard about Jesus live in this area. It has the greatest physical and spiritual need, most of the world's least reached peoples, and most of the world's governments that oppose Christianity. Yes, it includes countries making the front page of our newspapers, places where American soldiers are stationed or nearby—Iraq, Iran, Pakistan, and Afghanistan.

Countries in the 10/40 Window

North Africa: Morocco, Western Sahara, Mauritania, Niger, Chad, Sudan, Algeria, Libya, Egypt, Tunisia

Horn of Africa: Ethiopia, Eritrea, Djibouti

West Africa: Senegal, Mali, Guinea, Guinea-Bissau, Burkina Faso, Benin, Gambia

Mediterranean and Middle East: Greece, Portugal, Cyprus, Malta, Gibraltar, Turkey, Israel, Lebanon, Syria

Arabian Peninsula: Jordan, Iraq, Kuwait, Bahrain, Qatar, the United Arab Emirates, Oman, Yemen and Saudi Arabia

Central and South Asia: Iran, Pakistan, Afghanistan, Turkmenistan, Tajikistan, India, Nepal, Bangladesh, Bhutan

Southeast Asia: Myanmar (Burma), Thailand, Laos, Cambodia, Vietnam

East Asia: Philippines, China and Taiwan, North and South Korea, Japan

Looking Into the 10/40 Window . . .

Close to 65 percent of the world's people live in the 10/40 region. This area is the birthplace of Buddhism, Islam, Hinduism, and numerous other religions. What do you suppose many of the people living here know about Jesus, the Christ? From absolutely nothing to very little. Even what they do know is probably erroneous.

If you've ever been in India, researched it, or heard from someone who has, you would know that about 81 percent of the people are Hindu, 13 percent are Muslim, about 2 percent are Christian, and the rest are other religions including Sikhism, Buddhism, and Jainism. To illustrate the absence of knowledge about Christ in that country, let me share what a pastor friend of mine named Samuel told me happened to him.

One day when Samuel was in a village in central India, he stepped out of the hot sun into one of the typical shops. On the wall-to-wall shelves, he saw big and little boxes, jars, and bottles with food and medicine. Bins of beans, bananas, plantains, and other produce were on the countertops. The shopkeeper came forward to see what my friend wanted to buy.

"Do you know Jesus?" Samuel asked.

Much to Samuel's amazement, the shopkeeper turned around to the items in the store to see if he had this "Jesus" in a box or bottle. Turning back to Samuel, he said, "No, I don't have it here. Tell me where I can get it, and I'll get it for you."

How do you respond to an answer like that? It hurts the heart. So many like him have never heard the name of Jesus or anything about the gospel message. What are the chances you or I, realistically, can reach people like this man in their homelands? Probably pretty slim.

What if this shopkeeper were to move here to the US? Maybe a relative already living here invited him to come. Maybe he saved enough money from his shop to leave the poverty of his country, hoping to build a new life in ours. This man from the other side of the world would be here among us, but he still wouldn't know who Jesus is. It is a fact that people like him are coming here every day. The world really has come to us. This shopkeeper may now live in your neighborhood.

... Into Our Neighborhoods

While taking my daily walk in my neighborhood, I encountered an older gentleman dressed in Indian garb who was also out walking. Waving to him, I stopped as he approached.

"Sir," I asked, "would you perhaps be from India?"

"Why yes, I am," he responded.

That was the beginning of our conversation about his homeland and his native city, Calcutta. He was here visiting his son, who had a very good job at a local pharmaceutical firm. I learned that my house was only about five blocks away from where his son and family lived. We chatted a bit, and then I pulled out a scrap of paper. I wrote my phone number on it. I invited him and his family to come to my house next Friday for tea. (Tea is very important in India, so it was a good way to start.)

How easy that was! Plus, it was the beginning of a great relationship. You should have seen the man and his family when they arrived. Smiles on all their faces. A gift for me. And an eagerness to become friends.

As we became acquainted, I used basically the same procedure as when I first met my international student friend Manzur. I asked them to tell me about their family, their religion, and their life in India. They, like most internationals living among us, were ready and anxious to find a true American friend. Quite naturally, as a part of getting to know them and they, me, the door was opening to share the gospel. Like Manzur, these new friends didn't have correct information about Jesus. They asked questions, and it was my privilege to answer them. Amazing and wonderful.

The Languages and Cultures of the United States

People of different cultures, nationalities, and ethnic groups live in every US city and most towns. The different languages they bring to a community will surprise you even more than their numbers. Take the shopkeeper from India as an example. He probably speaks English and at least two other languages, since India has 18 major languages and hundreds of dialects and tribal tongues. A well-educated person from the Middle East, on the other hand, will probably speak his family's language as well as his national language and either French or English or both.

These peoples of different cultures and languages, who have left their familiar lands to live among us, are often lonely, curious, and in need of an American friend. They are ready to relate to us, to try to communicate with us, and, if we are open, to become our friends. Rarely do they accurately understand our culture, our traditions, and our values, much less anything about our faith in Jesus Christ as the Son of God and Savior of the world. How difficult is it for us to connect with them here in our own neighborhoods as compared to going to their homelands to meet them and introduce them to Christ?

I'm told that there are 237 countries in our world. No, I didn't count them. (And it depends on who's counting as to how many there are.) If you go to the Internet, you can find all kinds of information on each one of them. Would you like to know about South Africa? Go to a search engine and find more than you could imagine. Try Indonesia or Nepal. Statistics, photos, maps, and all manner of other information are yours for the searching. But to really get to know a country and its people, you have to get to know someone who lives or lived there.

How many different ethnic groups are in your city or town? How many different languages do they represent? One way to find out is to look in the Yellow Pages under restaurants and count the different kinds. You won't get the total answer, but you'll have a good idea.

I did a little research on ethnic restaurants in my area. I discovered, much to my surprise, that two miles away, at a major intersection, are Japanese, Chinese, Mexican, Italian, and Greek restaurants. Going a mile further, I counted nine more ethnic restaurants: Russian, Ukrainian, Moroccan, Thai, Italian, Mexican, Japanese, Indian, and Chinese. I really hadn't noticed them until I started counting. What is amazing is that my corner of the world is in the middle of the United States, far from any coast.

Another way I've discovered to find statistics about internationals in our communities is through public schools. I walked across the street to talk with Ruth, my neighbor. She is the principal of a public school not far from my house. This grade school with 740 children has 100 kids who must have training in English as a second language, since they are new to the United States. They are from India, Mexico, Pakistan, some countries in Africa, and the Dominican Republic.

Checking with another grade school close to where I live, I found that 95 percent of the children attending there are minorities. Those children speak Yoruba (from Nigeria); Spanish (from Mexico and Latin America); Mandarin (from China); Bambara (from Mali); Tagalog (from the Philippines); Vietnamese (from Vietnam); Hindi, Tamil, and Sinhalese (from India); French (from Africa); Russian (from Chechnya); Mina (from West Africa); and Urdu (from Pakistan).

Let's say you research a school district and find 20 different nationalities represented in that district. Behind each child are parents. Behind each parent are grandparents, aunts, uncles, cousins, and more cousins. Some live here, but all will have relatives or friends back in their homeland.

Most of these families are larger, having more children, than most American families. Missing their large families back home, those living here often get together because of homeland tradition. They also enjoy having others to talk with in their native tongue, people who understand them and care about them. We can be modern William Careys right here in the USA by connecting with these children, parents, grandparents, aunts, uncles, and cousins.

Understanding Influence

Your influence over people of other nationalities is stronger than you may realize. People living in a new environment are much more open to hear about and accept Christ into their lives than they might be in their homeland. Did you know that in most Islamic countries it is against the law to convert to Christianity? Or that just a few years ago, opponents of Christianity in Sir Lanka, a predominately Buddhist country, tried to enact an anti-conversion law aimed at evangelical Christians. (The bill did not become law, because it was ruled unconstitutional by the country's Supreme Court.) Imagine the freedom and openness people from these nations feel in a country where they can learn about other religions without fear.

If they were still in their original country, social, family, and political pressure would probably prevent them from considering what you might have to tell them about Jesus. Here in the United States, they don't have those pressures, so they can more easily listen and respond to the gospel of Jesus Christ. Think about it. Not only is it easier for you because you don't have to go to the other side of the world to meet them, but it is also easier for you because they are more open to hearing from you right here in your country!

Do these people have influence with others of their culture or nation? Yes, both here and in their homeland. When they do understand Christianity or become Christians, they have a tremendous influence on their family here and also on their family back in their homeland. Most non-native people living here try to go home once a year or at least every other year. If they have Christ in their heart, they will want to share Him with the people they love just as we do. They are the ones, not you or me, who can most effectively take the gospel to Iran, Mexico, Senegal, Sri Lanka, or wherever their homeland is. They know the language. They know the people. They know the religion. And with Christ in their heart, they will want to be God's missionary to those they love. Your influence, combined with their influence, can have far-reaching effects.

I am working to get to know a young man from Senegal. He's a really nice guy. I met him at a local shop. After getting acquainted with him well enough, I invited him and a few other friends to my home for dinner. There is no place like home to be able to talk about the Lord.

This young man saw the pictures around my house. Discovering I had nine grandchildren, he was most interested in their pictures. The next time I went to the shop to see him, he handed me a picture of his little girl back in Senegal, saying, "Here is my daughter. Her name is Awa, and she is six years old. Now you have another grandchild."

What influence will I have on Awa? I don't know. Probably not much, but I am sending cards and notes to her from time to time. What influence will this young man have on his daughter Awa? As a father, he will have a lot. When he comes to Christ, and I pray he does, he can use his influence to help his daughter find the Lord. He can use his influence to help his other relatives in the capital city of Dakar find the saving grace of Jesus Christ.

Senegal, on the west coast of Africa, meant nothing to me until I met my new friend. I had to pull out my atlas to find it. I also had to read *Operation World* by Patrick Johnstone and Jason Mandryk to find that it is 92.07 percent Muslim, 4.76 percent Christian, and 2.97 percent traditional ethnic religions. French is the official language. Islam grew from about 45 percent of the population in 1900 to over 92 percent today. Senegal needs Christian missionaries. If I can reach my new friend with the love of Jesus, perhaps he can be one of those missionaries so desperately needed in Senegal.

I was talking to a man at church about reaching out to nationals of other countries. Our conversation stopped when he gasped and said, "I never realized it before, but where I work there are lots of people from other countries. Why, I imagine at least a third of them are from other countries."

He went on to tell me he worked as a greeter at a store. After some more discussion, he was anxious to go back to work so he could check on how many people from other countries actually do work with him. He had a new sense of his influence. It was right before him, but he never had realized it. It was like he suddenly received a revelation from the Lord that the world had come to him and that he was responsible to do something about it.

He left me that day wanting to start being the disciple the Lord needed in his store. As I was talking with him later, he told me about an Ethiopian he works with who just came to Christ. Of course, he was excited to tell me. He hadn't realized he could be used this way for the Lord.

Take a drive around the community where your church is located. You just might find Hispanics or Arabs or Japanese in the area. One church I know has discovered enough Hispanics within a half mile of the church building that they are starting a Spanish-speaking church in cooperation with another church on the other side of this community. Yes, some of Latin America has moved north, and this church has discovered its place among the nations.

Our world is just outside your door. Do the obvious, easy, first step on discovering it. Count the people of different nations you see. When you start looking, the Lord will help you find them. Afterwards He'll help you make a connection.

Something to Consider

Here are three great facts of our time:
- The decline of Western domination and moral influence
- The resurgence of the world's great religions
- The rise of global Christianity and its missionary task

Consider these important statistics about our changing world. Read each one carefully, think about it, pray about it, and try to figure out what it means to you as a twenty-first-century disciple.

1. There are nearly 6.7 billion people in our world.
    International Bulletin of Missionary Research, Vol. 32, No. 1 (January 2008); David Barrett & Todd Johnson
    http://www.gordonconwell.edu/ockenga/globalchristianity/resources.php;
    Web site for the Center for the Study of Global Christianity, Gordon-Conwell Theological Seminary

2. About 50 percent of the world's people are urban dwellers. By 2025, the percentage may increase to 58 percent.
   International Bulletin of Missionary Research, Vol. 32, No. 1 (January 2008);
   David Barrett & Todd Johnson
   http://www.gordonconwell.edu/ockenga/globalchristianity/resources.php;
   Web site for the Center for the Study of Global Christianity, Gordon-Conwell Theological Seminary

3. The five largest cities in the world are Tokyo, Mexico City, Mumbai (Bombay), Sào Paolo, and New York City.
   www.worldatlas.com/citypops.htm

4. Nearly 61 percent of the world's people live in Asia.
   Operation World, 21st Century Edition,
   Patrick Johnstone and Jason Mandryk (2001)

5. Just over 1 billion people live in absolute poverty. About 2.2 billion people do not have safe water to drink. About 2 billion people are undernourished, with 500 million of those on the verge of starvation.
   2001 *World Christian Trends*, William Carey Library;
   David Barrett & Todd Johnson;
   http://www.gordonconwell.edu/ockenga/globalchristianity/gd/gd18.pdf

6. Christianity (all kinds) is the world's largest religion, claiming about 2.2 billion adherents (about 33 percent of the world's population). Islam is the world's second largest religion, with about 1.4 billion adherents (20 percent); Hinduism is third with nearly 890 million. There are more than 760 million people considered nonreligious. Buddhism follows with about 390 million adherents.
   International Bulletin of Missionary Research, Vol. 32, No. 1 (January 2008);
   David Barrett & Todd Johnson
   http://www.gordonconwell.edu/ockenga/globalchristianity/resources.php;
   Web site for the Center for the Study of Global Christianity, Gordon-Conwell Theological Seminary

7. The number of evangelical Christians worldwide has grown remarkably since 1960, from 84.5 million to 420 million in 2000. Most of the growth has occurred in Latin America, Africa, and Asia. Christianity is stagnating in North America and the Pacific (i.e.: Australia, New Zealand) and rapidly declining in Europe.
    Operation World, 21ˢᵗ Century Edition,
    Patrick Johnstone and Jason Mandryk (2001)

8. Christians face limitations on religious freedom in at least 46 countries; in many cases this reaches the level of active oppression and persecution (jail, torture).
    Open Doors World Watch List, 2007, http://www.od.org

9. Two thousand years after Jesus gave His Great Commission, approximately 1.87 billion people have never heard of Jesus Christ (28 percent of the world today).
    International Bulletin of Missionary Research, Vol. 32, No. 1 (January 2008);
    David Barrett & Todd Johnson
    http://www.gordonconwell.edu/ockenga/globalchristianity/resources.php;
    Web site for the Center for the Study of Global Christianity, Gordon-Conwell Theological Seminary

10. Presently, more than 70 percent of Christian effort and ministry is directed at people who already profess to be Christians, while less than 5 percent of our total missionary activity is focused on those who have never once had a chance to hear about the good news of Jesus Christ.
    International Bulletin of Missionary Research, Vol. 32, No. 1 (January 2008);
    David Barrett & Todd Johnson
    http://www.gordonconwell.edu/ockenga/globalchristianity/resources.php;
    Web site for the Center for the Study of Global Christianity, Gordon-Conwell Theological Seminary

11. Non-Western, or majority-world, missionaries are now nearly equal in number to their Western counterparts, who number more than 112,000.
"The New Face of Missions," by Rob Moll;
http://www.ctlibrary.com/newsletter/newsletterarchives/2005-12-13.html

12. In a survey by George Barna, 75 percent of "born again" American Christians could not define the Great Commission.
Moody, April 1994, p. 60;
http://www.sermonillustrations.com/a-z/b/bible_ignorance_of.htm

Action Steps

Take a neighborhood walk and count the different nationalities or cultures you recognize. How many did you see?

_____

Go to a nationwide pharmacy and see how many languages are available for their prescriptions. How many are there?

_____

Drive around your church and count the different nationalities or cultures you see. How many did you notice?

_____

Share all of this information with your pastor and missions chairperson.

Pray, pray, pray about how you can have a part, be it large or small, in reaching some of these people who do not know Jesus our Savior. After all, who else really knows they are there?

Chapter 4

What Do You See?

Vision consists of the ability to see it, the faith to believe it, the courage to do it, and the hope to endure until it is done.
—James Ryle, president and founder of Truth*Works* Ministries

I was invited to speak to a church group of senior citizens one evening at a nearby restaurant. The buffet looked so good. Yummy fried chicken plus roast beef, pork chops, fish, and all those salads. Various breads, unusual vegetables, and of course those scrumptious desserts caught our eyes. We chose our food, got our drinks, and headed to a private room for our meeting. We were engaged in the great American way to get together—good food, good fellowship, and good relationship.

When it was time for me to speak, I started with a question. "Did you by chance notice the servers at the buffet? You know, those people that were replenishing the food platters? What nationalities are they?"

The room became strangely silent. Not one had an answer. One fellow did try to twist his head to see through the door, but it didn't work.

"I talked with one of them, the young man who was bringing those fresh trays of meats. Nice guy. He is from Mexico, and his English isn't all that wonderful. I asked him what city he is from, and he told me Mexico City. That's over 2,000 miles from here. He went on to say that he has a wife and two babies there, and he is sending his money home each week. He works two jobs—this one and one at the McDonald's down the street."

The blank looks on their faces showed me they had no idea where I was going with this point. I had their attention.

"One of the lessons the Lord is teaching me is to see the world through His eyes. If Jesus had come into this buffet with us today, what would He have seen? Would He have seen the servers and talked with them? Or would a fresh tray of meat have been His main interest?" I saw some head nods. I was beginning to get through.

"Jesus seemed to connect with people wherever He went. He saw the blind men and asked, 'What do you want me to do for you?' (Matthew 20:32). When He saw the funeral procession of the widow's only son and saw her broken heart, His heart hurt too. Those connections were a big part of His ministry. Remember this one? 'Jesus went out and saw a tax collector by the name of Levi sitting at his tax booth. "Follow me," Jesus said to him (Luke 5:27).' 'Then He turned to His disciples and said privately, "Blessed are the eyes that see what you see"' (Luke 10:23)."

At that point, the people with me in the restaurant realized that they hadn't even looked at the servers. They were so intent on loading their plates with such great food that those serving them weren't important. Several of them came to me afterwards and thanked me for helping them see people in a new perspective.

Eyes of Compassion

It is time to start looking at the people in your world, people who need your eyes of compassion.

Are you in the habit of not paying attention to the opportunities to connect to those around you? We Americans have programmed ourselves to take care of our problems, look straight ahead, and not be sidetracked. But it is time for you to meet the people of other nations right there in the community in which you live and work.

Where do you start? Start in your own area. Maybe a house down the street from you just sold. Your new neighbor could be a good place to begin. A plate of cookies and an invitation to come to your house and visit you? Sure, you could try that. Why not?

Seeing people as Jesus does includes seeing everyone. What about the people who knock on your door to sell you something? You may discover that salespeople—insurance, real estate, carpet, Girl Scouts, or whatever—are easy to approach. After all, they come to see you about something they want you to buy. They are in your territory. If you invite them, they may come into your house and sit in your living room. After you realize that Jesus wants you to see them as He would see them, it isn't difficult to turn the conversation the direction you want it to go. (I'll show you how in chapter 10, "How Do I Start?").

Have you tried connecting with the people you meet in stores? A young man at the eyeglass center was helping me pick out frames. Seeing him through the eyes of Christ, I looked for a way to turn the conversation the direction I wanted. It wasn't difficult. I asked him his name. It was Joshua. I simply asked him why his parents chose that name. His answer?

"My parents are Christians." He didn't say he was. He did say, however, that he had recently moved to my town and was looking for some way to connect.

Looks like the Lord had that meeting all set up for me. I am so glad He is teaching me to see people through His eyes of compassion. He can do the same for you.

This morning I was at a car rental shop. Instantly, I recognized that the proprietor was probably from another country. I simply asked him his name. His answer sounded like "Cmoe." (I probably didn't spell it right.)

It was easy to go to my next question. "OK, Cmoe, what country are you from?" Can you guess? I couldn't either, but it was Morocco. As our conversation continued I found out that he came to the United States when he was 14, he has lived in Michigan and Oklahoma, and he has a wife who likes living in Indiana.

My friend who had gone in the shop with me was listening intently. When we left, we started talking about this process, and how excited Cmoe was to have somebody interested in him.

Once you see how easy it is to start a conversation like this, it does become contagious and others want to try it too. Try it and see for yourself.

A pastor invited me to discuss his missions program. He was interested in what I do. He asked me numerous questions. I steered the conversation to the host of internationals now among us. He let me talk about the Mexicans and other Hispanics in our town. I brought up the Chinese and then the Haitians. But when I mentioned Muslims, his response was, "There aren't any Muslims around here."

That pastor hadn't yet learned to see people through the eyes of Christ. I'm not sure he believed me when I told him 15,000 Muslims live in his city. There is also a huge mosque, but we didn't get to that.

This valuable lesson Jesus taught His disciples—seeing those around them with eyes of compassion—is for us today too. Look. Watch. Learn to see. Stand in the mall or a large department store and see, as Jesus did, the multitude. Yes, a multitude of people from many different cultures and stations in life is here. They are from everywhere, they live here now, and they will be staying.

Recently I joined a fitness club. Who was there to check me in? Abdel from Palestine. Another child of this world, made in the image of God, who has come to my neighborhood and has zero knowledge of the love of Christ. Abdel has grown up with the anger between the Israelis and

Palestinians hardening his heart. He liked talking with me. Why? Because I noticed him and took the time to listen.

This desire to meet people can be in your mind all the time. When you enter a store to buy the new mattress you need, just who might the Lord have waiting for you to talk to? You can have two agendas—to buy a mattress and to see if the clerk might be interested in the Lord.

Go to a restaurant. You can usually have time to talk with your server. Servers are real people. They have names and feelings. They usually have a purpose in their lives besides waiting on tables. Often they are students working as they are going through college. Sometimes they are immigrants who found that one job they could handle.

I was with some friends in a small Mexican restaurant. This restaurant was authentic. Real Mexican. Had that special smell of peppers and salsa. Our server was a young Mexican girl. I could hardly wait to talk with her. When I asked where she was from, she told us Cuidad Juarez. One of my friends jumped into the conversation. He told her that he had grown up in El Paso, just across the river from her city!

My friends are excited about making this discovery, because they go to that restaurant *muchos tiempos* (many times). They just hadn't realized until that moment how easy it is to see the servers there through the eyes of Christ. They now have the opportunity to take their new relationship on to the next level in future visits there.

Bound by Tradition

The Apostle Peter had to learn to see the world through the eyes of Jesus too. He had been with Jesus for three years, and he had learned much from Him. I can't even imagine the privilege it must have been to spend any time at all with the Lord, much less three years. I'd be happy with just an hour or even five minutes! But even after all that time, Peter still had a lesson to learn. It was a lesson in a dream, and it was about tradition.

Tradition! Oh, there's that word. Tradition, the way we've always done things. What we were taught earlier in life. What others expect of us.

Tradition had Peter bound to working only with Jews. But one day the Lord said it was time for him to change.

Peter was off by himself praying and minding his own business when the Lord dropped a bomb in front of him—actually it was a sheet containing all kinds of animals, reptiles, and birds—and told him he could eat those things. Tradition and Jewish law had told him he could not. They were unclean, and he was to leave them alone. The Lord was changing the rules. Through this vision, the Lord was telling Peter to associate with Gentiles. That was unheard of. Gentiles were people of different cultures. Gentiles were unclean, and so not acceptable to Jews.

"Surely not, Lord," said Peter.

He was afraid to move out of his tradition, his comfort zone. God knew, however, that it was time for Peter to see his world through the eyes of Jesus Christ, through eyes of compassion. It was time to look at people differently.

The Lord was saying something like, "Come on, Peter. Open your eyes. Start looking around you. Things have changed since I was walking around with you. Now that I am back with my Father in heaven, this is a new day. See these people? Sure they are different, but I love them too. I don't have favorites. I want people of every nation, every tribe, and every tongue to know me. And Peter, you can start making that happen." (I've paraphrased these words from Acts 10. Please check them out for yourself.)

If Peter or one of the other disciples had not started sharing about Jesus with Gentiles, you and I might not have heard the message of salvation. How glad I am that Peter learned to see the world through the eyes of Jesus Christ and told us in the Scriptures to do the same.

The love of God is for *all* people, not just a select few. That's what Peter learned. That's what you are learning.

It's not just for those who look like you and who talk your language. You are a part of a big family, the family of God. Your everyday existence is full of opportunities for seeing and responding to the world as Christ did. You can learn to extend His love, often and regularly, to those who do not know Him.

Tradition! It can keep you from seeing people. It can scare you from talking. If the people you encounter aren't like you and you don't know them, then they don't count, right? Just walk on by. Turn the other way. Be busy. Tradition! The way you've been taught. Beware of strangers. Watch out. Be careful. They aren't your kind. They aren't dressed the way you are.

But the people in those clothes you don't like just might be people who need you. Look at the one sitting next to you with a pierced tongue or a nose ring. Ah, tradition! Look at what is holding you back from connecting with that person.

There are times when it isn't skin color or dress or language that prompts us to see others through the eyes of Christ. Sometimes it can be pain or anguish on a face or in a response that might alert us to people's need. We can learn to see that too.

Jesus saw a father's distress. His daughter had died and he was hurting. Jesus stopped and spent some time with him, healed his daughter, and changed the look on the man's face to joy and happiness (Matthew 9:18–26). He saw a widow who had just lost her only son. His heart went out to her, and He said, "Don't cry." Jesus gave the son back to his mother (Luke 7:13–14).

An Open Door

I was having a problem with pain in my leg at night, which kept me from sleeping. It was time to do something about it, so I got in my car and started searching for a doctor's office. I found one a couple of miles from my house and went in.

Nobody was in the waiting room. The receptionist took me right in. After I told the doctor my problem and he set about to help me, he asked me what I do each day.

That is a fantastic question. You can do all kinds of things with it. Of course you can just say, "I work at an office" or "I work in a factory" or "I'm retired" or "I am a stay-at-home mom." If you respond with the ordinary, expected answer, then that is usually the end of the conversation. The alternative is to give an answer that is going to make someone curious enough to ask more questions. That's my approach, and here is why. It gives you a wonderful opportunity to lead the conversation where you want it to go. You can even talk about the Lord and what He means to you.

You can't do that? Need help? You might say something like this: "I work at an office, but what I enjoy each day is relating to people." Instead of saying "relating to people," you might say something else that is unusual but meaningful to you. The one you are speaking with will probably ask you what you mean by that statement, and away you can go in the direction you want the conversation to head.

Or try this one. "I've discovered a new vocation besides my job." The person you are talking with will ask you what that is. Maybe you answer, "I want to make people smile." Or maybe, "I'm going in a new direction."

"What's that?" the person will ask.

"I'm volunteering at the homeless shelter" or "I'm leading my children (or grandchildren) to find ways to change the world" are just a few responses to keep the conversation going. You can come up with any number of answers that will lead the conversation where you want it to go. Of course, you have to think about it and plan a few good answers ahead of time.

I say, "I'm a writer and speaker." That always brings on the next question, "What do you write or speak about?" I could say that I write Christian books, but it works best to create curiosity, to prompt the one I'm reaching out to ask me another question. For example, I might say, "I write about how we can make a difference in this world and have fun doing it." That's just enough to bring on more questions.

As I am leading the conversation toward my love for Christ and what He's doing in my life, I am watching for facial expressions. What would the Lord have me see in this person? Is this one a Christian? Happy or struggling with life? Big problems? What are the expressions on that one's face telling me?

As I answered my doctor's question that day, I saw pain on his face. It wasn't long before he started telling me about his hurt. He and his wife just recently had a baby with severe health challenges. Since the baby's birth everything else had gone wrong too, including losing patients because he couldn't be at the office all the time as he once had been. He started telling me the whole sad story.

If Jesus were here, He could heal the baby. I couldn't. But what I could do was ask him if I could pray with him. I did, right there in his office. And he was grateful.

I never dreamed I would be praying with a doctor in his office when I left the house that day. That's not why I went there, but that is what happened. The Lord gave me an open door, and I went in. I prayed for that doctor because the Lord let me see him through the eyes of Christ. The Lord gave me His compassion for him. I go back regularly to see him and pray with him now too.

The First Step

It is amazing what you can see and do when you begin to see through Jesus's eyes. It's a different world. People are different. They are individuals, not just figures in a crowd. They have feelings, problems, and pains. When you use Jesus's eyes, you begin to see everything around you in a different light. You begin to care. You begin to have the Lord's kind of compassion.

It looks like the Lord can use you after all. Of course He can. He even used a deceitful tax collector, people with leprosy, fishermen, and "bad women."

Here's your first step. Take some time to practice seeing how many different kinds of people are around you. Notice them. Watch for minor details that speak volumes. Analyze who they might be, what problems they might have, and what you could talk to them about. What nonverbal gestures do they have? Just use your eyes. Let your view of them rest in your heart. Even though you don't know them and probably never will, pray for them. They are important to Jesus. That makes them important to you. Start practicing seeing the world as Christ would see it. Eyes like Christ's. It certainly adds purpose to your life.

In the coming chapters, we'll be working on the next step of finding a place in your heart for the people you are seeing. You do have a big heart, don't you? The Lord will make it bigger, just the way He wants it. Your eyes like Christ's. Your heart like Christ's.

Something to Consider

How many people has Jesus shown you this week?

_____

Whom did you see today? What do you think their problems might be?

_____

_____

_____

_____

Pray for the people you remember seeing in the last few days.

Actions Steps

Write out an opening line to start a friendly conversation with a stranger. Think about how you will take the conversation in the direction you want it to go.

_____

_____

_____

_____

_____

Memorize it.

Write statements that will get the people you are seeing to ask you questions.

_____

_____

_____

_____

_____

_____

Chapter 5

. . . .

Reality Check

Bless the Lord, *O my soul: and all that is within me, bless his holy name.*
—Psalm 103:1 KJV

. . . .

Before you think about more deeply what you can or should say to those people you are beginning to see, take a moment to think about all the Lord gives you *because you are His child*. What do you have that those who don't know Christ are missing out on? Let's count them.

God's Blessings in Your Life

• **He forgives all of your sins.** This is number one. Everyone sins. I've sinned. You've sinned. Now look what Paul says:

> *Since we've compiled this long and sorry record as sinners and proved that we are utterly incapable of living the glorious lives God wills for us, God did it for us. Out of sheer generosity he put us in right standing with himself. A pure gift. He got us out of the mess we're in and restored us to where he always wanted us to be. And he did it by means of Jesus Christ.*
> —Romans 3:23–24 *The Message*

Forgiveness is the number one privilege. When God forgives your sins, He places you in His family. He becomes your heavenly Father. Actually, He is your "Abba" Father, a tender and attentive dad. He is always ready to forgive you when you ask Him.

He also *forgets* your sins. That's better than you can probably do with them! Listen:

> *He doesn't endlessly nag and scold, nor hold grudges forever. He doesn't treat us as our sins deserve, nor pay us back in full for our wrongs…and as far as sunrise is from sunset, he has separated us from our sins.*
> —Psalm 103:9–10,12 *The Message*

• **He promises you eternal life.** Jesus is in heaven preparing a place for you. He is getting it ready. Here's how He describes this privilege:

> *"You trust God, don't you? Trust me. There is plenty of room for you in my Father's home. If that weren't so, would I have told you that I'm on my way to get a room ready for you? And if I'm on my way to get your room ready, I'll come back and get you so you can live where I live."*
> —John 14:1–4 *The Message*

One of the best-known promises in the Bible is this, "For God so loved the world that he gave his one and only Son, that whoever believes in him shall not perish but have eternal life" (John 3:16). And here it is again. "I tell you the truth, whoever hears my word and believes him who sent me has eternal life" (John 5:24). How wonderful that you and I have His promise of eternal life.

Other religions are on the merit system. Islam, Buddhism, Sikhism, and other religions require you to do a certain amount of good things in order to get into their heaven. You won't know if you will make it until you get to heaven's door. We Christians have the promise and the gift of eternal life with the Father, the Son Jesus, and the Holy Spirit forever. What a gift!

• **He is always with you.** Morning, noon, evening, and night, He never leaves you. After He gave His Great Commission, Jesus said, "And surely I am with you always, to the very end of the age" (Matthew 28:20). You can communicate with Jesus any time you want to. He is always available. If you think you are not communicating, it is because you are not listening. It's not His fault. He is always with you.

He goes with you everywhere you go. He's your traveling companion, your helper. It takes some time to realize Jesus goes with you everywhere you go. But He does. You just have to recognize it. He is in the car with you when you are driving. He goes to the store with you. Of course, He goes to work with you. He is closer than your cell phone. He is always with you. He, through the Holy Spirit, is with you wherever you go.

• **He crowns you with love and compassion.** Through Him you overcome your meanness! What a blessing that He takes all your desires for self-glory and turns them into love, mercy, and compassion. He certainly makes a much better person out of you than you could do by yourself. He "crowns you with love and compassion" (Psalm 103:4).

• **He fills your life with good things.** What are the important things you have? No, not the house and the car. It's family and friends. How precious your family is—parents, siblings, children, and grandchildren. And what about your Christian friends? It seems like when you move to another location, you just double the number of your friends instead of losing any. Having moved twice in my life, I have discovered it is a special treat to go back and visit those "old" friends.

Jokingly I say that they think I walk on water, but I don't stay so long that they see that I can't.

It is wonderful to have people who love you, family and friends who call you friend and stick by you like a sister or brother. Their friendship surrounds you. It can comfort you when you need comforting. It can support you when you need support. And best of all, these people love you in spite of your shortcomings. Yes, he "satisfies your desires with good things" (Psalm 103:5)

• **He hears you when you call.** You can't get out of His range and you never have to pay roaming charges for calling Him. Even when you forget, He is beside you. When you call upon Him in distress, He is always ready—no answering machines, no extra charges. Your cell phone may sometimes be out of range, but your God is always available to answer your call. "Never will I leave you, never will I forsake you" (Hebrews 13:5).

• **He has a purpose for your life.** Most of us ask sometime in our life, "Why am I here? Why am I me? How did I happen?" I don't know the answers, but I do know you are here for the Lord's purpose in your life. He made you for His purpose. He has plans for you. "'For I know the plans I have for you,' declares the LORD, 'plans to prosper you and not to harm you, plans to give you hope and a future'" (Jeremiah 29:11). Isn't it great to know you have someone infinitely smarter than you working out the plan for your life?

• **He is your greatest joy.** "The joy of the Lord is your strength" (Nehemiah 8:10). "Shout with joy to God, all the earth" (Psalm 66:1). The Psalms are filled with references to joy. As you read them and experience God's presence, your heart is filled and overflowing with joy. What in this whole world could possibly give you greater joy than what you have through the blessed favor of being a chosen child of God?

• **He renews your spirit when you are down.** Yes, you have times when you are discouraged, have the blues, or feel dejected. How can you regain your footing on solid ground again? What can renew the right spirit within you? The joy of the Lord. The presence of the Lord. The promises of the Lord. The comfort of the Lord. The assurance of the Lord. Read the Psalms. They can always lift your spirits and plant your feet again on the Rock.

> *He gives strength to the weary and increases the power of the weak. Even youths grow tired and weary, and young men stumble and fall; but those who hope in the LORD will renew their strength. They will soar on wings like eagles; they will run and not grow weary, they will walk and not be faint.*
> —Isaiah 40:29–31

• **He fills you with His Holy Spirit.** It was the Apostle Peter who said, "Repent and be baptized, everyone of you, in the name of Jesus Christ for the forgiveness of your sins. And you will receive the gift of the Holy Spirit" (Acts 2:38). Jesus promised the presence and gift of the Holy Spirit. What power, unlimited power, if you think about it! You need all the help you can get, and the Holy Spirit wants to help and guide you.

• **He surrounds you with assurance, direction, and protection.** Here is a Scripture verse that can help you understand His special care for you. "See, I am sending an angel ahead of you to guard you along the way and to bring you to the place I have prepared" (Exodus 23:20). It's always good to know an angel is around to look out for you. You need that. So do I. He gives direction too. "Whether you turn to the right or to the left, your ears will hear a voice behind you, saying, 'This is the way; walk in it'" (Isaiah 30:21). You just might catch me looking over my shoulder to see the source of that voice, thanking Him for His care and direction.

• **You know Jesus.** "Jesus answered, 'I am the way and the truth and the life. No one comes to the Father except through me'" (John 14:6). You know Jesus, and you have to know Him to know the Father. This is the foundation for who you are, whom you serve, and where you will spend eternity.

I met a young man in Laos recently. I asked him if he knew Jesus. "No," he replied, "who is he?" Can you imagine life without knowing Jesus, much less never having heard His name? You and I have the joy of knowing this Jesus and enjoying His fellowship, care, love, and salvation. What if someone had never told you and me about Jesus?

Yes, you have the privileges that come with knowing **Almighty God**. He is your healer, deliverer, guide, and friend. He fills you with joy as you read His Word. He gives you challenges and helps you with them. He is with you in trouble, sickness, and death; He is with you not just in good times but all the time. He is giving you eternal life with Him. And the list goes on and on. What a mighty God you have! Wow! Just look at all He is for you. Incomprehensible and wonderful. Enough to change the world.

His Desire for You

Look at the list again, all those gifts He has given you. So what is your part in this relationship with God? Accept Him. Love Him. Be obedient. Go make disciples. Share the good news.

Ah, but there is more. Peer down the road ahead. You'll see unheard of opportunities, fun, joy, blessings, and things you could never dream of just waiting for you. You want a life with purpose and adventure? Want to get started on the real stuff of being a Christian? Keep reading. God has His plans for you. Your comfort zone is only a small place in a big world. It's time to step out of it.

Something to Consider

Think about all the blessings the Lord has given you. Yes, all of them. As you remember them, list them below.

_____

_____

_____

_____

_____

_____

_____

_____

What do you *really* want to do with your life?
Pray about it.

Action Steps

Is your life purpose-driven?
Write your life purpose on a piece of paper.
Date it and put it in your Bible.
Share it with your spouse or a trusted friend.

Chapter 6

Becoming a Twenty-First-Century Disciple of Jesus

I will instruct you and teach you in the way you should go; I will counsel you and watch over you.
—Psalm 32:8

My name isn't Peter, James, or John. I'm just me. So Jesus, how do I become Your disciple today, here in my town, without You around to teach me? Where do I start? I don't know how to do this, so You'll need to teach me.

This prayer is the door-opener to a path of surprising joy and fulfillment. Using these or your own words, you can affirm your desire to be the Lord's disciple and share with Him your dependence on Him to teach you. Stop right now, put a marker in this book, and spend some time in conversation with Jesus. Confirm with Him your desire to be His disciple in this twenty-first century. Share with Him the fears, anxieties, and problems you think you will have in doing this.

Are your knees sore from kneeling in prayer? No? You prayed, but you didn't get on your knees to do it? For me, getting on my knees is the best position to learn what the Lord wants. Sometimes Jesus got on His knees when He prayed to His Father in heaven. Sometimes He didn't.

Physical position in prayer isn't important, but heart position is. Just talk to the Master Teacher, and tell Him all that is on your heart. He will be delighted to hear from you.

Walking with Jesus One Step at a Time

When Jesus was here on the earth, His disciples walked with Him. He led them one step at a time, and they learned from Him as they walked and talked. Not too difficult, right?

Becoming a twenty-first-century disciple isn't going to be too difficult for you either. There aren't too many steps, and you can take them one at a time so you don't get overwhelmed. As you do, you will be learning the skill of faith-risk. You will be bold enough to take each step and yet perceptive enough to know when to slow down or back off.

Ready? Let's get started. Here are the basic steps. Each one will be explained more fully in the upcoming chapters.

1. **Choose to follow.** The first step is to choose to follow Jesus. When you follow someone, you go where that person takes you. You don't argue or try to take the lead. You follow.

Notice how simple it was when Jesus met His disciples and they chose to follow Him. The Book of Matthew records what happened when Jesus met Peter and Andrew. "Come, follow me," Jesus said, "and I will make you fishers of men" (Matthew 4:19). At once they left their nets and followed Him.

Now it's your turn. Respond to His "follow me" right now. Say something to Him out loud. Here's an example. "OK, Lord. Whatever. Here I am. I'm ready to start."

That was easy, right? The first step was only one breath!

2. **See what He sees.** If He's leading and you're following, you have the luxury of looking at the sights and not

worrying about choosing the path. What is there to see as you go to work, to the grocery store, to the golf course, and to the gym? Look at the world, and try to imagine what His eyes are focusing on as you go about your daily activities.

When Jesus was here on earth, the Scriptures say that He repeatedly saw the crowds, the multitudes, (Matthew 5:1, 9:36; Mark 6:34). He must have been walking where a lot of people were. Don't worry about where you're walking. He'll take you to the people that He wants you to see. Your job is to follow Him and focus on what's in front of and on each side of you. What do you see? What do you think He is seeing? Ask Him as you're walking along, and He'll tell you what He sees.

3. Feel what He feels. Scripture says that when Jesus saw people, it affected Him (for example, Matthew 9:36). He didn't just see people. He saw them and had compassion on them. They affected Him. They got to His heart. When they hurt, He hurt. He connected with what He saw.

The first four books of the New Testament contain many accounts in which Jesus saw hurting people. He saw ten lepers who asked for healing. He saw a boy possessed by a demon. He saw blind Bartimaeus and later two blind men on the road to Jericho. He met a woman of Samaria.

In each of these encounters, Jesus understood how these people were feeling. He connected with their pain. He was so upset about the death of Lazarus that He wept (John 11:35).

That's your next step—to feel what Jesus feels. To be affected by what affects Him. You will learn from Him as you connect your heart to what your eyes see.

4. Make contact. Next comes the step that probably scares you the most, the initial contact. What do you say to a stranger that is different from what you'd say to a good friend? Just be yourself. Act natural. Be friendly and polite.

Did Jesus bring all the people He saw to their knees in the prayer of salvation on the first encounter? Hardly. Learn from Him how to make contact and with whom. Realize that with some people you see and connect with, you may have the opportunity to build a relationship over time. With others, you may not.

Just knowing that it is not your "job" to pour the plan of salvation into everyone's lap should calm some of your fear. Yes, there are bold, assertive, and frightening ways to reach out to people, but there are easier ways too. Go for the easier ways. You're just starting, remember?

5. Build relationships. Next, you will try to build relationships with the people Jesus shows you as you are walking with Him. As you develop a relationship with someone, you learn to trust each other. When someone trusts you and sees what's in your heart and your life, that person can ask you questions. You can ask that person questions too. You can listen to stories, and you can tell some of your own.

When someone you are building a relationship with is in need, you can talk about how the Lord has helped you. You can share a story or two of what the Lord has done in your life. No need to be pushy or try to solve that person's problems. Your stories, your words, are seed. When seed hits the ground, God can do what He does best—create something from it.

Once you have planted seed in someone's life, you will want to water and tend it. If the seed were corn, for example you would expect to wait weeks and months before the harvest. The seed of the gospel may come up quickly, or it may take months and years. Learn to water and tend it. Eventually there will be a harvest.

Five steps. That's all. Since you are still reading this book, you've probably already taken the first two. You are walking with Jesus, and you are beginning to see what He sees.

How to Spell Success

As you walk with Jesus as His twenty-first-century disciple, you'll also discover your connection to His first-century disciples—people like Peter, James, and John. In other words, sometimes you will be able to do great things for God, and other times you will not. Sometimes your faith may be fantastic, and other times it may be weak and not productive.

Was Jesus "successful" 100 percent of the time He reached out? Hardly, if success only means acceptance! And what about His disciples? Even less!

Do you know the story of the rich young man that came to Jesus? He chose *not* to follow Jesus. Was that Jesus's failure? Not at all. He presented the message to the young man, but the young man chose not to accept it (Luke 18:18–30).

Here are two more cases when people could have become Jesus's disciples but chose not to. In one account, Jesus asked a man to follow Him, but the man replied, "Lord, first let me go and bury my father." Another man said, "I will follow you, Lord; but first…" (see Luke 9:59–62).

Do you know the story in which Jesus's disciples couldn't help the boy with a demon? They said, "Why couldn't we drive it out?" (Matthew 17:14–19). Jesus used that encounter to teach them. He uses our encounters to teach us. Some are glowing successes and we rejoice, and others fall flat. We are to learn from our Teacher—learn from each encounter just what Jesus wants us to learn.

You could equate Jesus's teaching us as we walk along with Him to teaching a child to ride a bicycle. "Get up on the seat. Now start moving your legs and pumping those wheels. Watch where you are going!" you say. About that time, the child loses his balance and falls.

Is that a disaster? No. You say, "Good job. You're coming along. Let's try again." You know that the child will succeed as he continues to try. He won't ever ride a bicycle, however, if he gives up after the first or even the second time he falls.

Keeping at it, he will soon be riding it everywhere. And remember, even an experienced bike rider hits a bump and falls occasionally.

Sometimes Jesus tells us, as we're walking along behind Him, just to do what we can, say what we can, and if it is not accepted, move on. He knows that not everyone will listen. Not everyone wants to know about Him. Not everyone has time to be bothered.

So what is our response supposed to be when we are rejected?

In one story, Jesus sent 72 of His disciples out to witness in various towns and villages. He told them something like this: "If they accept you, that is wonderful. If they don't, shake the dust off your feet and go on to the next place." They did it. And they returned full of joy. That made Jesus full of joy too.

We don't know how many people refused them and how many accepted them, but we know they returned to Him full of joy. Can that be all there is to "success" in God's eyes? His disciples simply doing what Jesus says and coming back to Him full of joy? Yes. You don't have to be successful, but you do have to be faithful. It's called obedience.

Think about what else was happening in that story. Those 72 disciples were getting a vision for their part of the world. That, too, was part of God's plan for them.

As a twenty-first-century disciple, you are developing a world vision too. You are learning to see differently and think differently. You are learning to seize the opportunities to reach people and to show them love and compassion.

Jesus's faith was tested. All kinds of questions were asked of Him, and He was rejected by many people, but those things didn't stop Him. He was faithful to His Father. He taught His disciples how to handle testing too. He said to "love the Lord your God with all your heart and with all your soul and with all your mind" and then to "love your neighbor as yourself" (Matthew 22:37–40).

That rule for discipleship still applies. Remember it when you are tested or when you think you were not successful. I think Jesus had a statement of faith too that kept Him on track in spite of opposition. It seemed to be: "Seek first his kingdom and his righteousness" (Matthew 6:33).

What Does Jesus Want from His Twenty-First-Century Disciples?

First, fellowship. The Lord wants fellowship with you. Look back at that prayer you prayed with Him at the beginning of this chapter. Fellowship with Him comes before anything else. He wants you to be with Him and enjoy Him, not just follow Him blindly. His commandment, "Love the Lord your God with all your heart and with all your soul and with all your mind" (Matthew 22:37), is because He wants that kind of a relationship with you.

Remember the Garden of Eden, where God walked with Adam and Eve in the cool of the day? What a relationship that must have been until they blew it. He still wants that kind of relationship. He wants to walk with you. He wants your fellowship.

Next, God wants you to walk with Jesus, follow Jesus's example, and learn from Him. Read about all He did, and try to do the same. Follow His teachings. Study them and learn from Him. Put them in first place in your heart.

The Lord will help you to:
- Do what He wants you to do
- Be what He wants you to be
- Say what He wants you to say
- Give what He wants you to give
- Go where He wants you to go

Your time here on earth is for a purpose. You have been created for His purpose. If you ever wondered what your purpose is, now you know. Peter, James, John, Andrew, Philip, and all the other first-century disciples aren't here. You are. You are Jesus's chosen twenty-first-century disciple.

Take a good look in the mirror—it's you. God delights in doing surprising things, things that we cannot imagine. What do you think God might be starting to do through you today? You might just be surprised.

Something to Consider

Write your personal commitment to Jesus Christ, Almighty God, here.

_____

_____

_____

_____

_____

_____

Answer the following questions with a *yes* or a *no.*

Am I willing to be an ambassador for Jesus Christ? _____

Am I willing to be a disciple for Jesus Christ? _____

Am I willing to be a servant for Jesus Christ? _____

Am I willing to be a slave for Jesus Christ? _____

Action Steps

Ask a couple of friends to be your prayer support. You will be praying for your new relationships, and you need prayer partners to pray with you and for you.

Write the following in your Bible or on a piece of paper. Sign and date it. Place it in your Bible.

I will do what He wants me to do.
I will be what He wants me to be.
I will say what He wants me to say.
I will give what He wants me to give.
I will go where He wants me to go.

Chapter 7

What Breaks Your Heart?

Although the world is full of suffering, it is also full of the overcoming of it.
—Helen Keller

I have a virus. I got it in China several years ago. It has affected my heart, and I've discovered it can be contagious. I even want it to be contagious. Does that frighten you? My virus isn't a deadly disease. It is "missions," or you might say it is reaching people who don't know Jesus. And I do want it to be contagious.

All through the Bible, from the beginning to the end, is the message that all nations are to be brought to the Lord. It isn't a last minute plan. It isn't just Jesus saying, "Oh, yes, I forgot to tell you to go throughout all the world and make disciples." It isn't the great suggestion. It is the Great Commission. Go! Make disciples! Baptize them! Teach them! And Jesus will go with you always.

When Bob Pierce, founder of World Vision, visited Korea in the early 1950s, he saw so much poverty, sickness, and lostness—people who had no knowledge of God and Jesus—that it broke his heart. He jotted down these words in his Bible: *Let my heart be broken by the things that break the heart of God*. It became his life motto. It is mine as well. I feel the words must have come from the heart of Jesus.

Compassion takes on a new meaning when you let your heart respond to what your eyes see. Scripture says that Jesus saw the multitudes and had compassion on them. I haven't always seen multitudes like that. A long line of people or a crowd tends to make me want to go the other way, to get out of there.

What about you? Are you prone to see the multitudes and just wish they would get out of your way? You could get out of the grocery store faster if all those people weren't in front of you. You could have a good seat in the restaurant and ease that hunger pain in your stomach if so many people weren't already ahead of you.

Heart Surgery

The Lord may have to work on your heart, just as He had to work on Bob Pierce's and on mine. He may have to give you a heart like His, one that sees people and feels their pain. One that responds to a person and recognizes a relationship to that person. Your heart will be able to respond like Jesus when you can see that most of the people on the street, those in the grocery and restaurant, your new neighbors, and others you meet may have no understanding of salvation and no hope of eternal life. That is, unless someone such as you cares enough to reach out to them in love.

Jesus wants us to have a heart that looks into a face and is concerned for the person's wellbeing. Compassion. You can have that kind of heart. Let Him do the surgery.

"OK, Lord," you reply to what your eyes see and your heart feels. "I can't change them. It's up to you to do that."

He replies by telling you that He uses everyday, ordinary people, people right where you live, to be His twenty-first-century disciples. He doesn't plan to come back here and walk around healing and preaching again. He commissions new disciples to work for Him. You are one of His new disciples.

Training Camp

To be His disciple, you need direction. You need to get your orders from the Lord. You have to do it His way, in His timing, and with the opportunities He makes for you. What you say and do is not all up to you. Being His disciple is a team effort. God calls the shots, and you do the work.

"So, Lord, what do You want? Time together in the mornings, for a starter? Wait a minute. You know I'm always in a hurry when I get up. I have my job to do and my list of things to get started on. You really want me to stop and talk to You first? Before I get started on my day? Why, Lord? Oh, because You have instructions for me, and You want me to do things Your way. I see. You want me to read some of Your Word too. Well, OK, but you know I don't have very long. So your Word has instructions for me? And if I don't understand it all, you won't call me a dummy? You'll just tell me that if I continue reading, eventually I will understand it? OK. I can do that."

Can you have that conversation with God? Try it now. Then try the next one as well.

"You say the Bible is a playbook like those pro football players have to study? Yeah, I've heard of them. The players learn the terms, the plays, what works, and what doesn't work from the playbook. So you're calling the Bible a playbook? OK, Lord. I'll read it and study your plans. I want to win these games. Maybe I can learn to be a pro for you like a football player does for his coach."

Prayer, communication with the Coach, becomes a regular discipline for your daily spiritual fitness training. Even if you say your heart is already in good shape with the Lord, I say you still have to work to keep it in shape each day. Your heart can get out of shape so fast! It requires daily training and retraining, like a pro football player trains for every game. And why? So you can play your best.

When you are in shape, you can say to Him, "Where's the game today, Lord?" This is when expectations of the day ahead get exciting. These conversations bring divine appointments for you and produce the results He wants. And those appointments lead to even more intimate conversations with Him.

When you are in shape, your conversations with the Lord can include talking to Him about some of those people you've been meeting. Maybe you're a list maker. Make a list of the people God is putting into your life who need His touch. Go over the list with God. He has time. He's interested in your thoughts.

Has tradition kept you from praying in this way? You may have to learn how to pray all over again. You may find that your prayers are beginning to be filled with the needs of others more than your own. That's great. He can change your heart, and He can give you compassion. Love and compassion are two of the special gifts He has for all of His children.

When I wake each morning, I pray that my heart will be broken again that day so that I can be useful to my Lord.

Heartbreaking Stories

A Veteran

A man I met recently broke my heart. As a young man, he was going to be a preacher. Then the US Army set him down right in the middle of Vietnam. He was assigned to be a tunnel rat. Tunnel rats were soldiers chosen to find the Vietcong tunnels, go into them, and clean out the enemy. A scary job at best. An extremely dangerous job. He was captured and kept in captivity for months until he found a way to escape. When he made his way back to his outfit, he was placed right back into the tunnel assignment.

Here he is years later, mad at God for the whole thing. "Why did God let that happen to me?" he asks.

When I try to answer, he's not ready to listen. So what does that do to my heart? I know there is an answer. I know the Lord can take all of that anger and give him peace and joy. I know that Almighty God can restore him to fullness and make a great disciple out of him yet. This one is going to take time, and building the relationship is the key. It's enough for right now to feel the brokenness in his heart and add his pain to mine.

A Crowd

I was in Mumbai (Bombay), India, to visit an outreach ministry in that country. Usually I stay away from big crowds, but that time was different. The final afternoon of my trip was open for killing time before going to the airport to catch my flight home. Walking down the streets, going in those little shops to see what bargains they had or what might interest me, was my focus that afternoon. There were certainly all kinds of things, and the shopkeepers were ready to sell me any and everything.

I had just climbed up the steps to cross the street over a pedestrian bridge when a loud whistle started screeching. What happened next was an amazing sight for this American's eyes. People came pouring out of every door, filling the sidewalks and even the street. They were everywhere. Never had I seen such a crowd. Well, maybe after a big football game, but this was different. It didn't take long for me to understand that the whistle was telling them that their workday was ended. They could go home.

I watched as they hurried along on their way. To me they were a huge crowd, a multitude. At that moment, the Lord reminded me of when He saw the multitudes and had compassion on them. Looking at all those people hurrying in all directions through eyes of compassion made me pause. My heart said to me, *Just how many of these people have ever heard the name of Jesus?* They were Hindus or Muslims, Jains or Sikhs, animists or Buddhists. The vast majority of them, I knew, had no—zero—knowledge of Jesus and His love for them, of His desire to care for them, and of His ability to bring them into a relationship with our heavenly Father.

So what did the sight of those people evoke in me? I understood that I couldn't reach them. I couldn't speak their language. I certainly wouldn't be allowed to preach to them. But the Lord pierced my heart with His compassion. As I looked at them, tears began coursing down my face. My heart was aching.

"I can't tell them. What can I do, Father? What is the purpose of this sight to me?"

Yes, the Lord put the people of India on my heart that day, and we talked about it many times after that moment in our prayer conversations. It wasn't long before He gave me a way to reach them. I began supporting an Indian Christian leader whose purpose is to reach his people, show them the way to eternal life, plant churches among them, and disciple them. God gave me an answer, but first He had to break my heart with the sight of a crowd, a multitude.

A Prison

I was in a prison in Latvia back in 1991. No, no. I wasn't a prisoner. I was a guest. I was supposed to speak to the prisoners. The warden, a short, decisive man, was showing me around and explaining everything. He was showing me the workstations, the exercise yard, and the heavy security area. I was attentive, although this certainly wasn't my favorite place to be. The prisoners were dressed in their prison garb, and all had their heads shaved. Some were doing the various jobs they were assigned. Others looked like they were waiting for the end of the world.

The warden turned to me unexpectedly and said, "I once believed that Communism was the ultimate answer for life. The leaders of the Communist Party here in Latvia led us to believe that we were going to have a great life. I did everything they told me to. And now it is over. Finished. Everything is changed. Would you tell me about Christianity? How is it different? Is it a good plan?"

Now that's a question! I was glad he asked me, but just the question made my heart break. All those years following the wrong leaders, going down the wrong trail. But it did give me hope since he was asking the right question now. And yes, because I had prepared in advance, I was ready and able to give the answer he needed.

The Evening News

Your heartbreaks probably won't be in India or Latvia or any other foreign country, although they may be. The Lord will give you a heart of compassion as you seek His will and desire to do His work right where you live, in your community. That's the beginning.

If you're open to it, there are times when just reading the newspaper or listening to the evening news can break your heart. How does it affect you when you read that millions of our nation's babies die each year from abortion? How does your heart break when you hear about men and women casting aside the privilege of a Christian family to enter into an unholy homosexual relationship? What about the news of a drunk driver killing a family in a wreck? Or a troubled teenager gunning down his classmates?

Here in the United States we have plenty of evil and tragedy. We have devised all kinds of ways to break God's heart. Do any of these things break your heart?

Father, let us have Your love and compassion. Help our hearts to be in tune with You. Let our hearts be broken by the things that break Your heart. Help us to be useful to You as twenty-first-century disciples—like Peter or James or John were—but today, here, in our part of the world.

Something to Consider

Talk to God. Consider praying these words: "Let my heart be broken by the things that break Your heart, God." Write them down and paste them on your mirror or cupboard.

List those things that break your heart.

_____

_____

_____

_____

_____

_____

_____

_____

Action Steps

Practice seeing the multitudes and checking your feelings of compassion. Where are the multitudes in your world?

_____

_____

_____

Write down the new people the Lord showed you today to add to your prayer list.

_____

_____

_____

_____

_____

_____

_____

Find someone who will pray with you about the multitudes who don't know the Lord.

Chapter 8

What's Your Story?

Be good news before you speak good news.
—Steve Sjogren, author, church planter, pastor

Maybe you haven't realized it, but you have one of the most precious stories ever heard. It's not one your mom or dad told you. It's not about your ancestors. This story is the one about you and God.

Remember how you became a Christian? How God found you? What you said and what you felt when you repented and God forgave all of your sins? Yes, He forgave all of them. Even the ones that you didn't want anyone to know about. He knows everything about you, and He saw your repentant heart. He forgave you, made you His child, and brought you into His family. Now you are a child of God. A changed person. It's an amazing story, and it's yours.

Christianity is the only religion that offers this precious relationship with the one true God, available to all who seek Him and find Him. We Christians are people with amazing stories. Because your story happened only to you, no one can share it as you can.

Sharing your story is part of those steps in becoming a twenty-first-century disciple. As you listen to the story of your new friends, you earn the right to tell yours. It's all part of building relationships.

Write It

If you haven't already, it's time to write your story. It's important. Maybe it happened 20 years ago, or maybe it happened last week. The time doesn't matter, but the parts of the story do.

If you became a Christian a long time ago, remembering the details will be harder but not impossible. The details may be important too. If it happened more recently, your task will be easier. Whichever the case, it's important to write out your story with as many details as you can. Time has a way of erasing our memories, but when we take the time to write our stories down, we capture them.

The first part of your story is who you were before you met the Lord. What were you doing, and how were you living? What was your life like? How did you feel? Lost? Hopeless? Angry? Take some time to reflect on those facts and feelings. Write about them. As you do, you'll be amazed at the drama in your own life.

The next part of your story is how Christ found you. Where were you when He spoke to you and told you He wanted to change your life? What unusual circumstances surrounded His being able to find you, reach you? What brought you to that place?

Then there are the transformation details—how He actually changed your life. What comfort did He give you? Did you feel the release of your sins and your past? Was the change like night to day, or did it come on more gradually? What changed first? Feelings? Attitudes? Life circumstances? Values?

You probably can remember a few instances when Jesus helped you at a point of real need in your life. Think about sickness, loss of a job, an accident or near accident, or even a death. Take your pick of the best, because when you start thinking about how He has helped you since you became His child, you'll find that you have several more parts to your story. Write the best ones down. They'll be useful as you talk to the new people the Lord is going to put in your path.

Your stories are tools you can use as you learn to be a disciple. Be ready to talk about your experiences with God. Little ones or big ones, it doesn't matter. They are your stories, and people want to know about you.

Where are you spiritually right now? Is anything in your life still in the process of changing? How are you different? What do you do differently now? These details are part of your story as well. Once you start, they'll flow into your mind like rushing waters—rivers of blessings.

Your story is unique. It's undeniable and irrefutable. It's what happened to you in your life, and it's awe-inspiring. Cherish it. Memorize the details. And get ready to share what the Lord has done for you in all its glory.

Get Ready to Tell It

The act of writing your story will make you better prepared to tell it. You will be ready when the right time comes, and it will come. There will be a time when your story is the perfect answer. Your new friends will want to know about you. It isn't sermons or scriptures that are going to make them listen. It's what has happened to you.

One of the best ways for people you meet to become interested in knowing Christ is to hear your personal story. They want to know what God means to you and how you are different because you are a follower of Christ. They don't want a lecture. They don't want a guilt trip. No condemning, please. They just want to know why He is important to you.

If I were with you right now and I could sense that the time was right, I would tell you the following face to face.

I'm not, but I think you'll appreciate what I'm about to share. Notice how I share my details. It may give you ideas on how to share your story.

My Story

I'd like to tell you my story. Maybe you can relate. Maybe you can only listen and be amazed with me. Here it is.

I grew up in a Christian family. My parents and my brother and I went to church every Sunday morning and evening and every Wednesday night as well. It wasn't wonderful for me. Our church was very legalistic and critical, and I put up with it because I had no choice.

Over the years as I went to church without really wanting to, turmoil built up in my heart. At age 15, I wanted what I wanted. I was angry—angry with the church, angry with God, and angry with my parents. This religious lifestyle was too much, and I wanted to do my own thing.

Then one day (and how blessed that word *then* is) I went to a church service in another city. *Then* I realized it was time for me to give my heart to God. That moment wasn't like when Jesus spoke to Paul on the road to Damascus. No blinding light. No burning bush like Moses had. I just felt a gentle nudging in my heart that was telling me I needed to surrender myself to the Lord, that God had a purpose for my life. I went forward to the altar at the front of the church, knelt, and asked the Lord to be my Savior. *Then* the Lord forgave my anger, my sins, and my self-righteousness. *Then* He took me into His family.

Then my desires changed. My life-purpose changed. I wanted to be a Christian and make my life count for God. I wanted God's love and peace in my heart, and I had it.

No trumpets sounded inside my head or in the church that day. No public display of emotion. I just felt the special, inner peace that the Lord gives to those who surrender to Him. It was a feeling I will never forget.

Since then, He has led me and directed my life into places and situations that I could never have imagined. I often question where I would be today if I had not had that precious, God-appointed time and opportunity to invite God into my heart and my soul.

What do you think? Did you connect with my story? I hope so. My story, your story, any story is not a one-size-fits-all. You have to select the details to fit the person you are sharing it with.

Lora's Story

Lora, my friend, has a story that she tells to help others connect with the Lord. Here is how she tells her story in her own words.

I always thought there was a God. I thought I believed in Jesus Christ. I led a good life, a normal life with a normal family when I was young—until I turned 16. That was when my parents divorced, and I turned to sex, drugs, stealing, and everything that came with teenage rebellion.

That part of my life ended when I became pregnant with my now 5-year-old son. The drugs, stealing, and lies stopped. I was good again. Still, something was not right. I had a child, a man, a house, a job, a car, money, everything I could want, but I was so empty. I had been empty since before I was 16. Something was missing.

I tried to find myself within myself, but to no avail. I was still empty. When my relationship with my son's father ended, I was even emptier than before. I felt hopeless.

I had thought about God before, but I thought there were better answers, like finding myself. Then I started to pay attention to people who seemed happy and content, those who had a purpose. It seemed all of those people had Christ in their heart and in their life. At last, I understood.

Jesus Christ died on the cross, of His own will, for my sins. He alone could be my salvation. The Son of God, my Lord.

From that very moment, my entire heart changed. I felt honestly and completely free. My whole perspective on life changed too. Things that seemed so important before were trivial. God gave me my heart and soul back.

I still have concerns and doubts, but I know I'm in love with my Father in heaven, my God, and His Son Jesus Christ. I can't give you the definition of salvation, but I do believe I feel it in my heart and my very soul. I feel Christ in my heart, really feel Him with me. And I have an overwhelming feeling to speak out for God, to tell my experiences, not for myself, but so I can persuade others to come to Christ. I have a passion, if Christ will guide me, to help God build His church.

That's Lora's story. You can feel her honesty. As she is able to tell it to others, they can relate to her and ask questions about their own searching.

Brad's Story
My friend Brad has a great story too. It's one of those before-and-after stories. He didn't know the Lord or what blessings were available to him until he hit a brick wall. Here's his story.

I was raised in a church-going family, so when I was young I thought I was a Christian. I knew the rituals. When I went away to college in 1963, science told me that it was the only explanation of life that I needed. So I said I was an atheist. There was no absolute truth, just our culture saying what was right or wrong. All values were relative.

After graduation, I landed a good job. I got married and had two children. Everything was going well. I didn't need God. For 20 years, it seemed like I was well in control.

Then my wife left. I didn't know what to do.

Finally, I tried praying—for the first time in my life. One August night in 1987, as I knelt down by my bedside to repeat my same prayer of several weeks, that my wife would come back home, I heard a voice, a clear voice. It said, "I am with you. I will lead you."

I was shocked. I couldn't believe it. I wasn't even a Christian. Who said that? "God, could that possibly be You?"

It was kind of strange. I always said I didn't need God, but something was tugging at me. I was beginning to believe that maybe there was a God after all. I'd go to church and weep unexplainably. Was it God's presence touching my heart?

I had to find out. I was struggling with the first real problem in my life, and I was totally lost at sea. I was desperate. One day I even went up to the front of the church to kneel at the altar. My head said, Don't do this. It's foolish. But my legs just took me up there. People prayed for me as the pianist sang, "At the end of broken dreams, people need the Lord." That song had my name all over it.

Not long after that time, my wife divorced me. I was still processing that strange voice that spoke to me in my prayers. I continued to search for an answer. Was it God, Jesus, an angel, or what? I joined a church membership class to find out what it was all about. By the time the speaker on evangelism came to the class, I was ready to go from door to door shouting: "Don't be a fool like I was for 42 years! There is a God! Jesus is real!" I couldn't believe myself.

Before God spoke to me, the Bible made no sense. Afterwards, the Word became flesh and poured into me, and began miraculous healing and growth in my life. Not long after that, He blessed me with a beautiful new marriage and a new, blended family.

More Stories—Something for Everyone

Just like you can't tell the story of how you became a Christian in the same way with everyone, you can't tell your other stories—the stories of how God has worked in your life—to everyone. I don't. I listen, and God tells me which ones are right for those I'm talking with. Some people need light stories, adventure stories. Others respond to tough stories.

If I need a funny story to share, I can tell about the time I was in China and the government official served me cobra soup and then asked me how I liked it. OK, you won't have that story, but you'll have your own funny ones and others from your times of trouble.

One of my stories I have ready to tell is about my husband's death. That was unexpected. That was really tough. He found out that he had stomach cancer, and, in 87 days, he was dead. Having gone through that experience, I can help people who are having problems with losing a loved one. They know I can understand.

I also have stories as to how the Lord has protected me in dangerous situations. One of those times was at the busy Mumbai international airport in the middle of the night. The Lord sent what I felt was an angel (no wings visible) to take care of me.

I can tell you about the times God gave me love and joy in difficult situations and how He got me started in writing and speaking. If you have time to listen, I have stories.

My friends have more stories too. Here's another one from Brad about his journey with the Lord.

Five years after my divorce, I realized the need to take another big step forward—surrender my "self" to God. I was fearful. Like Alice in Wonderland when she was shrinking, I wondered whether I would disappear if I let God take control of me. God walked with me through my fear. And guess what? I didn't disappear.

When I let God take control of me, my new, true self was never more fulfilled. I realized that all this fanfare of resistance and self-will was the protective device of my ego to keep my true self from emerging and being victorious. My "self" often deafened God's call. When the earplugs of "self" were removed, I started to hear His voice more clearly and to see His hand better at work. Pure, seeming coincidences start to happen; prayers were answered in miraculous ways.

Shortly, God connected me with Reverend Samuel Stephens and the India Gospel League, an overseas missions organization. Me, involved with overseas missions? Not likely. Then one day God told my wife and me, "Leave your home and go to the land I will show you." Well, we said yes and visited India. Our hearts were broken for the lost in India. We came home, said yes again, and began a prayer and support group for the work in India.

I was struggling with being a leader. God wasn't finished. Due to the growth of the India Gospel League, Reverend Stephens asked me to work as Interim Director here in the United States. "Please, God. I'm a follower, not a leader. I don't have that ability. It's out of my comfort zone."

And God said to me again: "I am with you. I will lead you."

So what happened? Problems, situations, prayers, resolutions, problems, prayers, answers. Yes, it is totally exciting and a blessing to be used in God's work. I wonder, What does God have ahead for me to do?

God's Advertising Agency

We are like God's advertising agency. We promote God to others by the experiences we have in every area of our lives, both failures and successes. Through our life stories, we tell how He is with us in difficult times and how He gives us success when it seems impossible. We "market" God to the public. We work in God's advertising agency, and He blesses us with His love and tender care.

It's your life and your example that count, so get all of your stories ready. You will need them. The Lord is going to help you use them as you step out as His twenty-first-century disciple. Your stories are what will interest the people you encounter. Remember, people don't want your preaching. They simply want to know who the Lord is to you and what you have come through. They want to know why you are His disciple.

Now is the time to get ready for the questions about your life that people will ask you when you start talking to them. The questions will come. You'll repeat your stories many times over the years. Each time, you'll be blessed to see how your new friends listen. They'll catch a glimpse of how the Lord has blessed you and cared for you. Hopefully they will consider having a relationship with Jesus Christ too—sooner or later. The timing of that step is up to God. The telling of your story is up to you.

"Whatever you do, do it all for the glory of God" (1 Corinthians 10:31).

Whatever, Lord?

Yes, whatever!

Something to Consider

How would your family and friends describe your life before God showed up? _____

_____

_____

_____

_____

Who or what did God use to show you your need for Him?

_____

_____

_____

_____

How has God worked in your life since you made that commitment to Him?

_____

_____

_____

Are there special experiences or Scripture verses that God has used to bring you closer to Him? Why were they important?

_____

_____

Action Steps

Write your story of becoming a child of God. Work on telling it in a way that sounds good to people who don't know God as you do. Be careful not to use "Christian-ese," or words they would not understand. Do it now.

Practice telling your story in front of a mirror until you know how to say what you want to say. Memorize it.

Write stories about other significant times when God provided for you.

Chapter 9

Get Rid of Those Fears

"For I am the LORD, *your God, who takes hold of your right hand and says to you, Do not fear; I will help you."*
—Isaiah 41:13

So you're afraid? Join the club. Most of us are. The Lord's club teaches you how to overcome fear and enjoy every aspect of each encounter. After all, these encounters are divine appointments the Lord has arranged just for you, nobody else. Just you. You can do things that no one else can do. So let's deal with this fear thing.

The Peter Principle

First, let's talk about a disciple in the Bible who had a problem with fear. It was that mighty apostle, Peter. Before he became that mighty apostle, he was just an ordinary guy. No one was more ordinary than a fisherman in those days. He, like many others, worked for the local fish market.

One day a stranger came by the lake while Peter was at work. He asked Peter to come with Him—follow Him. Now why should Peter do that? The stranger must have been compelling. Something about Him made Peter join His team.

Jesus told Peter that He would make him a fisher of men. "Come, follow me," He said to Peter and a few others, "and I will make you fishers of men." (See Matthew 4:19). Look at Jesus's words again. *"Come, follow me, and I will make you..."* Stop there. Jesus said He would "make" him. In other words, what Jesus had in mind wasn't about who Peter *was* but what Jesus would *make* of him.

Yes, that's what we need. We need to be *made*. We need to be empowered and trained. We don't know how to reach people, to be "fishers of men." Like Peter, we are probably better at catching fish. So we need the touch of Jesus to make us, to teach us, to mold us into disciples, twenty-first-century disciples.

Can you pray these words right now? *"Yes! Come on, Jesus. Here I am. Make me a fisher of men—and women too!"*

Great. That's a start. Let's see what happened to Peter later on.

Peter was close to Jesus during the three years of Jesus's ministry on earth, so you know the Lord was working on him. Jesus made sure that Peter was there when He healed the sick, restored sight to the blind, fed the multitude of 5,000, and fed another multitude of 4,000 (with no food court around). Peter was there when Jesus raised Lazarus from the dead. Peter was even one of the three disciples Jesus took with Him onto the Mount of Transfiguration. Jesus must have had high hopes for Peter and could see in Peter's future far more than what Peter could see about himself and his abilities.

When Jesus gathered His disciples around for that last special supper, Peter was there at the table. By that time, he had started to ask Jesus some pointed questions. That night, as Jesus was washing His disciples' feet for them, Peter questioned if Jesus should wash his feet. After all, Jesus was the teacher and Peter was only a disciple. Peter just didn't understand everything yet, and Jesus was OK with his question. It was a good one.

Later that night, Peter and two other disciples, James and John, were in the Garden of Gethsemane with Jesus. The

Lord was in agony. He knew He was going to be crucified. But Peter and his friends were worn out and sleepy. They really weren't there when Jesus needed them. Not awake to what was going on.

When another follower of Jesus, Judas, came to the garden with the palace guard to betray Jesus, Peter pulled out his sword and took a whack at one of the guards, cutting off his ear. Brave, right? Peter made a mistake, but it didn't upset Jesus. Peter still had some things to learn. Jesus healed the ear of the guard to make up for Peter's mistake. Then Peter had to watch as Jesus was led away.

Next came another problem. The Roman soldiers took Jesus as their prisoner. Where was Peter, this guy who had been with Jesus constantly for three years? He was keeping his distance. He was fearful. He didn't know what to do, so he backed off, staying out of sight.

Have you ever been fearful of talking about Jesus? Peter was fearful that night. When a servant girl asked him some questions about Jesus, he was afraid to answer truthfully. He refused to acknowledge that he was even a member of Jesus's team. "Not me," he said three different times that night. Then he was gone. Hiding. Fear was controlling him.

Where was Peter during the crucifixion? No mention of him. Where was he afterwards, when Jesus was laid in the tomb? Not around then either. Fear seemed to have gotten the best of him.

But that's not the end of the story of Peter. It couldn't be, because Jesus had called him to be a fisher of men. Look what happened after Jesus was resurrected and back with His disciples.

Jesus challenged Peter, asking, "Do you truly love me?"

Peter gave the right answer that time. "Yes, Lord, you know that I love you."

Jesus asked him the same question three times, and three times Peter answered in the same way. (See John 21:15–19.)

Peter was stating the principle on which he would live the rest of his life. How did Jesus respond? He reinstated Peter as His disciple.

Everyone makes mistakes. Everyone is afraid. And everyone needs to know that there's going to be another chance, many more chances to act as a disciple of the greatest One who ever lived.

Peter: A Changed Man

In His last moments on earth, Jesus told all His disciples that they would receive power from the Holy Spirit. Peter needed a little power. No, Peter needed a lot of power. Fear had gotten the best of him there in the garden and later too. He knew he needed the help of the Lord to conquer fear. Lots of help.

Yes, the Lord had His plans for Peter. On the day of Pentecost, everything changed for him. A crowd had gathered, a huge crowd. Some were amazed by what they were hearing. Some were perplexed. Questions came from every corner. Who was this One named Jesus? Confusion.

Wait. There is more to the story.

"Then Peter stood up" (Acts 2:14). Did you hear that? *Peter stood up.* He stood up in front of a huge crowd. More than 3,000 people. The one standing up was Peter, the disciple who had been afraid to acknowledge Jesus to a servant girl who spoke to him outside of the place where Jesus was being questioned by the authorities. On the day of Pentecost, Peter stood up in front of thousands of people!

Look what happened next. He started speaking (See Acts 2:14.) *Peter, the fearful, was preaching!* Peter, an ordinary guy. Because of God's power, Peter went from being a coward to a great evangelist. About 3,000 people accepted his message and were baptized that very day.

Do you just suppose that Peter was surprised? He didn't go to seminary between the crucifixion and

Pentecost. He probably didn't have a three-point sermon carefully prepared for that occasion. This crowd was undoubtedly more people than he had ever spoken to in his whole life.

What happened to Peter? It's really simple. The message that Jesus put in his heart was *greater* than the fear in his mind.

Peter had a marvelous message that had to be delivered to the people. He understood that he, despite all his failings and weaknesses, was God's instrument. The people in front of him didn't know what had been going on. They needed to know. He knew, and he had to tell them. Their salvation that day depended on him delivering the message.

Peter had something important to tell the people in front of him. You do too.

Later on Peter wrote a letter to tell Christians how to be ready in any situation. In 1 Peter 2:9, he said,

> *But you are a chosen people, a royal priesthood, a holy nation, a people belonging to God, that you may declare the praises of him who called you out of darkness into his wonderful light.*

Peter was basically saying, "Prepare for action. The game of life is going on, and you have a part to play in it."

"Who, Me?" Moses

Do you know the story of Moses? He was the one God chose to lead the Israelites out of Egypt. He didn't want to do it. After all, an estimated two million-plus Israelites were living in Egypt at the time. When we read Moses's life story, we can understand why he didn't want to do what God asked him to do. He was timid; he was shy; he claimed to have a speech impediment; and he was afraid. He had actually been hiding from Pharaoh in the desert for 40 years. Here's what happened.

The Lord told Moses that He wanted him to lead the entire nation of Israel out of captivity. Moses' first response to the Lord was, "Who am I?"

Yes, I can relate to that. You probably can too.

"I will be with you," the Lord replied.

Fear still controlled Moses, so he said, "What if they do not believe me or listen to me?"

The Lord continued with His request, so Moses replied, "O Lord, I have never been eloquent, neither in the past nor since you have spoken to your servant. I am slow of speech and tongue."

"Who gave man his mouth?" the Lord answered.

"O Lord, please send someone else to do it," Moses pleaded. (See Exodus 3:4–4:17.)

Imagine the scene. Moses was arguing with the Lord and making Him angry. The Lord understood his fears, so He told Moses that he could take his brother Aaron with him. The assignment, however, was still for Moses to do.

Have you ever tried any of those excuses of Moses?

I have. They didn't work. Then I came across an old saying, "What do I have to lose? What do I have to offer?" That helped me put the Lord's requests for me in perspective.

Obedience Is God's Measure of Success

"What if I try and fail?" you ask.

Is failure what you're afraid of? Don't expect all of your encounters with those who don't know Christ to be easy or successful. They won't be. Instead, write out a new definition of success. Do it right now. Mine goes something like this: *Do what God says to do when He says to do it, and let Him do the rest.* When He gives you a nudge, an idea, respond to it.

I remember my husband telling a young man at the time of his ordination into ministry, "Enrique, you don't have to be successful, but you do have to be obedient."

Some people you try to connect with won't tell you no to your face. Instead, they will find a way to avoid you. My friend Karen asked a couple to go with her to see the movie *The Passion of the Christ*. They didn't exactly refuse. They chose to be busy instead. That was safe, because everybody's busy, right?

Not everyone is interested in Jesus. People weren't in New Testament times, and they aren't today either. You can't let the fear of rejection stop you from doing what you are called to do by God.

A star baseball player is doing great if his batting average is around .300 or above. That means 300 hits out of 1,000 at-bats. That rate of success would not be very good if it were for anything but baseball. Do you know what happens on those other times the star baseball player tries to hit the ball? He's there. He swings. Those other 700 tries are strikeouts, fly outs, or groundouts—not hits.

Look at Jesus's ministry. He had encounters when He was rejected. Look at the story about a rich young ruler (Matthew 19:16–29). That young man might have done great things for the Lord. No, he decided that following Christ was too costly for him. He'd do his own thing. Rejection.

Here's another thought. We don't really know how many people Jesus called to be His disciples. We only know the stories of those who said yes. We can only wonder how many said, "No, not me."

What about the disciple named Judas? Jesus invested in him, made him one of the Twelve, and Judas let him down. Worse than that. You know the story.

Jesus didn't have a high success rate with His neighbors in Nazareth either. He went home for a visit, began to teach, and they took offense at Him. They asked, "Isn't this the carpenter? Isn't this Mary's son and the brother of James, Joseph, Judas, and Simon? Aren't his sisters here with us?" (Mark 6:3).

As the disciples chose to overcome their fears and not keep track of their batting average, they got with it. Andrew was always bringing people to Christ. He was the one who brought to Jesus the little boy that had the five loaves and two fish that Jesus used to feed the multitude. Philip talked to the Ethiopian eunuch, an important official in his country. The man listened and was baptized. John spent the rest of his life telling all who would listen to him about Jesus. He even spent his last days writing the message we know as Revelation while he was imprisoned on an island.

So what if you are not always successful? It is nothing to be afraid of. Jesus is not counting on a predetermined success rate for you—a hit or an out. He's counting on your obedience. *You* present the challenge to those you meet. *They* decide the response. You are only responsible for presenting the challenge.

Fear Factor

Even so, other fears keep popping into your head. Questions like, "What will people think of me doing this?" Or maybe "What if someone asks me a question that I can't answer?"

Who puts these questions in your head? It is Satan. He trains his demons to whisper in your ear and get your attention. Aren't these fear factors just that—factors that keep us from being obedient? And look at the questions themselves. They're focused on the speaker and not the hearer. You, not them.

King David in the Old Testament voiced the greatness of God and used it to drive away fear. The writer of Hebrews quotes David like this, "The Lord is my helper; I will not be afraid. What can man do to me?" (Hebrews 13:6).

To put it in baseball terms, the way to overcome fear is just to swing the bat. God is with you—your thoughts and your words. He will be your helper. You have nothing to fear except your fear. And you can't get a hit unless you try.

Every time you swing the bat, you get better at it. Your swing gets smoother. Your muscles get stronger. Your eyesight gets keener. Your determination to connect with the ball increases. I wish I could tell you what your success rate is going to be, but I can't. Besides, your job is to swing and let God keep the stats.

Not everyone we share with will come to faith. That's not how it happened for Jesus either. Instead, here's what He promises. He says He will be with us, and He will be our encourager. "Never will I leave you; never will I forsake you" (Hebrews 13:5).

Talking to others, reaching out to them in love, gets easier as you keep working at it. If you start by asking the waitress her name and find out she enjoyed connecting with you, you'll find you can do it again. Not hard at all. Sometimes the conversation goes on, and sometimes that is the end of it. Whichever happens, you'll start being able to discern her interest. You'll learn how better to start a conversation with her next time. Your adequacy is not the point. Your inadequacy is not the point. God's adequacy *is* the point. And He is right there with you.

You're in Good Company

So you're still afraid? Relax. You're in good company. Glad to have you on board with the rest of the twenty-first-century disciples.

You will overcome fear as you follow the Lord day by day and with each encounter. Stack up those encounters. Keep working at it. Find out about the people God puts into your daily life—who they are, where they come from, and what they want in life. It is surprising how many stoic faces suddenly turn to smiles when they find out that you really are interested in them. And remember, there is more to each encounter than you can see. Not one is an accident. All of them are God's divine appointments.

The Apostle Paul says in Romans 1:16, "I am not ashamed of the gospel, because it is the power of God for the salvation of everyone who believes." That Scripture can keep you moving forward. Paul also tells us in Colossians 3:17, "Whatever you do, whether in word or deed, do it all in the name of the Lord Jesus."

You probably won't do as much as Peter did in his lifetime. You don't have to. Peter isn't here. You are. Just do what you can for your Lord in this twenty-first century.

Something to Consider

What is your greatest fear? Write it out and pray about it. Turn it over to God._____

_____

_____

_____

What two Scripture verses strengthen you? Write them here and memorize them. _____

_____

_____

_____

_____

_____

_____

_____

Action Steps

Put a picture of Jesus in your wallet where you can see it every time you open it.

Put a Scripture message on your cell phone's opening screen.

Start a conversation with one stranger today, and then see if you are as fearful as you were at first. Write the person's name down and how you feel about your time together.

_____

_____

_____

_____

_____

_____

Go for three more. It gets easier. Remember: The message that Jesus puts in your heart is greater than the fear in your mind.

Chapter 10

. . . .
. . . .
. . . .
. . . .

How Do I Start?

Start by doing what's necessary; then do what's possible; and suddenly you are doing the impossible.
—St. Francis of Assisi

. . . .
. . . .
. . . .
. . . .

You've done a reality check on what God has done for you. You've chosen to follow Jesus and see what He sees and feel what He feels. You've written your story. You've recalled other stories of how God has intervened in your life. Now you are ready to connect with the internationals in your area. How do you start?

The Universal Language

A warm and genuine smile on your face is essential. The first thing you do is smile. It will give you a good start. If you're not in the habit of smiling, start now. Look in the mirror. Is your smile appealing? It has to be. Work on it. A stone face is not appealing. A fake smile is even worse.

Flash your smile wherever you go—to the grocery, to the mall, to the ballpark. Who looks happy? Sad? Bored? Worried? Who looks a bit different? Are they from Mexico? Asia? Africa? It doesn't matter. They may not have been in your area very long, and they might be lonely. Everyone can use a smile. Give it to them.

You see a stranger in front of you. Look at that person as you've learned, through the eyes of Christ, and smile. Maybe he's an American, but he has a different skin tone. You don't know. Maybe she's a Muslim woman, since she wears a *burka* on her head.

How do you know if this person is someone God wants you to connect with? You don't know for sure. Just give it a try. Give your best smile.

What's in a Name?

The next step beyond a smile is a bit of conversation. Where do you begin? Here are some easy ways. I'll give you the easiest way first.

If the person happens to have a name badge, start there. Let's say his badge says *Aaron*.

"Aaron. That is a great name. I've always liked it. How did you happen to be named Aaron?"

If the name has any biblical significance to him, he will probably tell you. If it doesn't, then you can say something about the story of Aaron in the Bible and watch his face for signs of interest. If the signs are there that you can continue, you can then take the conversation further. Since you just talked about a Bible story, you can ask where he goes to church and why. From his response and interest, you can tell if you should go further or move on.

What if the person's name is Sherry or Suzie? No biblical significance there. Say something nice about that name, perhaps telling about someone you know with that same name who is a wonderful Christian.

I met a man at an electronics store. His badge spelled ATM. I asked him if that was his name or if he was giving money away if I had the right password. That brought a laugh and his response, that his name really was Atm (pronounced *A'tem*). He seemed happy to tell me more about himself. Further conversation revealed that he was from Bangladesh and was the manager of the store. He had a wife and baby at home. They had been in this country for a couple of years and had all intentions of staying.

Amandou worked at a fast-food restaurant. It was easy to ask about his name because it too was so unusual. He told me he was from West Africa. I wanted to know more than that, so he added that he was from Senegal. His face lit up with delight that I had spoken to him rather than just picking up my order and going on my way. I had made a new friend that easily. After that day, every time I walked into the restaurant, he remembered my smile and our bits of conversation. His face always broke into a bright smile. I am learning to catch the signals people send me.

At a department store, I saw the badge of a young lady named Izeta. She, too, was delighted that I started a conversation. Izeta was from Bosnia. She had done quite well in mastering the English language. She asked me to come back and talk to her again.

One day I met Maria, a woman from Haiti. It was easy to ask her how long she had lived in our town, because her accent let me know she hadn't grown up there. She was glad I asked, and she started talking to me about Haiti.

Peter works at a restaurant I like to go to frequently. I started talking to him the first time I was there, and now it is fun to pick up the conversation each time I return. He's just an ordinary young man from our neighborhood, going to college and working part-time to pay his bills. It is fun to talk with him. We are now talking about his purpose in life plus what he wants to accomplish in the years he has ahead.

You know what I'm about to say. People like Atm, Amandou, Izeta, Maria, and Peter are all around all of us. Whether people are living in a culture that is foreign to them or close to home, they will appreciate your smile, words of conversation, and friendship.

Door-Openers

Have you ever run ahead to open a door for a stranger? What a great way to use your smile and have a chance to say a word. You may have no further conversation, but you will have added a spark, be it ever so small, to that person's day with your smile, your greeting, and your servant heart.

Here are some other "door-openers" to use when you are talking to people of other nationalities. Don't worry. They won't be offended. In fact, I always find them to be pleased. Each is a starting point that you can talk with someone about and then add other points of interest as the conversation develops.

The first door-opener is, "Have you been here in (name your city) very long?" Then you can ask, "What country are you from?" If you know where the country is, tell the person. If you don't know, ask. If you've been there, talk about it. If you can say sincerely that you might want to go there sometime, share that desire.

Here's another opening. "When did you come to the United States?" The person can usually tell you the year, sometimes even the month and the day. Most people who are from other countries keep close track of their time here because it's so important to them. Continuing on, you can ask about the person's homeland. "What is it like there? What is school like for the children?" Ask how grocery stores are different. Ask what the predominant religion is. And don't miss asking what the person's religion preference is.

Here's more. "What brought you to America? Do you like it here? Have you lived anywhere else?" This is the time to say, "Welcome to our city. I hope you like it here and are treated well."

Going On

If the door is still open, proceed. "Do you still have family in (name their country of origin)? Do you have any other family here? How long do you plan to stay here?" These starters may help draw the other person into a friendship.

Next comes a fun part. Say something like, "I'd like to hear more about your country. I'm really interested. Can we go get some coffee or a soda?" Maybe you can take the person to a coffee shop close by, or maybe set up a time to meet later. Give it a try. Why not?

One of my favorite questions is, "What do you do when you're not working here?" That question often brings more in-depth answers about the present and what the person wants to become some day. I have found that many of the waiters and waitresses in restaurants are in school or college working on their future. This discovery opens the door for even more in-depth conversation.

As your friendship develops, there's more. You can go on with something like, "How can I help you? Is everything working out for you OK here in our city?"

You can say, "Here's my phone number. Give me a call if you need help or would like someone to talk with. Can you give me your phone number too?"

What do you have to lose? And look at what you have to offer—Jesus and eternal life (when the time is right and the person is asking questions). The important thing at the moment is that you are on your way to developing a relationship, a friendship with someone who had been a perfect stranger to you.

One Christmas, I was in Detroit with my son and his family. When it was time to go home, my daughter-in-law took me to the airport. I got in line, checked in, and made my way to the gate. Waiting there among the others, I heard the agent call my name and ask me to come to the counter. *Why would that be?* I wondered. I thought everything was in order and I was all ready to go. I went to the counter as I had been requested to do.

"Donna Thomas?" the agent inquired.

"Yes, I'm Donna."

"You have been upgraded to first class."

What an unexpected and nice surprise. I took the boarding pass and didn't ask any questions.

Boarding the plane, I found seat 2A. Not hard to do. The man in 2B stepped out of my way so I could get in. After we were seated, we started the usual conversation…the weather, the plane, the trip. Since I was on my way there, I asked him why he was going to Indianapolis.

"I'm from Buffalo. I work for a copier company and have to be there on business. This happens about once a month or so." He then asked the most logical next question. "What do you do?"

I chose to answer him in such a way that he would ask me more questions. "I speak around the country some."

"Oh, really? What do you speak about?"

"I speak about finding the purpose of your life," I answered.

"I need to talk with you," he said instantly. "I am floundering with my purpose. How do I find it, and what makes life worthwhile?"

I had certainly never expected an answer just like that. The remainder of our time on the plane was spent talking about the Lord, getting rid of sin, finding direction from God, and walking forward in the purpose God has for him. He was so eager and asked so many questions, and before I knew it, he was ready for prayer. Yes, we prayed right there in First Class, row 2. He asked the Lord into his life, to give him purpose, and to help him to be the man he wants to be.

That was a wonderful divine appointment. Now I realize it wasn't the airline that upgraded me but the Lord. It was a joy to be used by the Lord in a place and a way I never suspected. (I would like to be upgraded again but it hasn't happened.)

You don't know where an encounter is going to lead. You only know that you are being obedient to the Lord. You might have a great opportunity to lead this new friend to the Lord some day. Then again, the person might not be ready. Your part is to take the initiative. This is seed-planting time.

Current News

Let's say you want to lead the conversation further with someone you've already talked with on a few occasions. A good way is by asking about a current item in the news, a book, or a movie. Try this: "What do you think about..." or "Did you hear the news about...?"

I had a good talk with Harold, who was working at a hotel, by using one of those questions. Yes, I learned, he was a Christian, and we had a great conversation. He also had some questions for me, and I was able to help him with those. I discovered that time, and you will too at times, that some people who respond to our questions are Christians. Some are not. Whether they are or not, most people are willing to talk, if only for a few minutes. They are willing to talk if we are willing to listen.

My friend Paula overheard someone use the title of a book to launch into an extended conversation during an airplane flight. There were empty seats on the flight, so one young woman from the rear of the plane came forward and asked a flight attendant if she could sit by her. The flight attendant was reading a book about the movie, *The Passion of the Christ.* She motioned to the woman to sit next to her. As she sat down, she asked the flight attendant about the movie and what she believed. Their conversation continued for the remainder of the trip. Paula said it was a beautiful example of a Christian taking an opportunity and sharing her thoughts and feelings about Christ with a stranger.

Here's another good conversation builder about something current in our culture. In fact, I had a clerk in a department store ask me this question: "Have you read that book that has been on the best-seller list for a couple of years called *The Purpose Driven Life* by Rick Warren?" You'd be surprised how many people know about that book and are interested in it. Just go on from there. Let them ask questions. Then ask if they have a purpose for their life. Even if they have not heard of it, the title may challenge them to ask questions about what it means. Either way, you win.

The Art of Listening

An important skill in building an interesting conversation is the art of listening. You do the listening. Listen to what your new friends are saying. Don't be in a hurry. Learn about them. Ask engaging questions. Listen to their answers. Hear their excitement. Relate to their disappointments. Find out what is important to them. Where do they hurt? Where are they happy? Challenge them to ask you questions, and answer their questions the best that you can. Yes, listen and don't preach. People won't listen to you unless they sense that you like them. And show love and compassion. That's what Jesus did.

At the end of a time of conversation with a friend, plan the next time you can get together. After you leave, you may want to write down everything you can remember for the next time. Store it in your heart. Take this new friend to the Lord in your prayers. You are on your way!

Be a Friend, Not a Salesperson

Have you heard of Mary Kay, Longaberger, Amway, or Pampered Chef? Someone sometime may have tried to sell you their products. These companies have a marketing and sales plan that uses everyday people to sell their products. They are always on the lookout for people to work for them. People choose to be salespeople for them in order to earn money. And then the training begins.

There is certainly nothing wrong with how these products are marketed and sold, but that approach is NOT what you are called to do. Being Christ's disciple does put you in a different position from the ordinary Joe or Susie.

You will need to be with people to make connections. But you are not there to "sell" them on Christianity. You are there to develop a friendship. As your friendship grows, the people you encounter will discover quite naturally that Christ is the center of your life. You can arrange times together to answer some of their questions about the value and importance of Christ to you, but you are not there to "sell them" on Christianity. You are there to be their friend and answer their questions about Christ when the right time comes.

Philip, the Deacon

Let me modernize the story about Philip in Acts 8:26–39 as an example of a disciple. A congregation had a problem. It needed a team to help with the church food program. The congregation had a business meeting and chose seven men to fill this need as deacons. Philip was a dedicated Christian, so he was named as one of the seven.

One day Philip felt the Lord telling him to go outside of his comfort zone into a different neighborhood. There he would find a man who needed him. Philip didn't know what all this meant, but he chose to obey. He went out looking for what God had in store for him, even going down a strange road. There he came upon a man sitting on a bench reading a Bible. That wasn't an everyday sight, so Philip realized that the Lord wanted him to talk to this man. Coming up to him, he asked a simple question, "Do you understand what you are reading?"

"How can I," the man said, "unless someone explains it to me?"

The man showed Philip the verse he was reading. Philip realized the Lord had brought him there for this purpose. He began with that very verse and went on to tell the man about Jesus. He told him that Jesus was the Savior and that He was able to help everyone, even today, all these years later.

Philip didn't stop there, as he saw that the man was eager to hear more. He continued to tell him about Jesus as Savior and how his personal life was changed as he followed Jesus. The man was amazed. He had never heard anything like that.

As they continued their discussion, the man said to Philip, "Look, I want this Jesus in my life too. I need Him and I want to know how I can connect with Him." Then Philip led the man in a prayer of repentance as he accepted the Lord as his Savior.

You've heard a similar story like this before. The story of Philip and the eunuch who was returning from Jerusalem to Ethiopia. Because of Philip's obedience to God, he led this man to Christ. Church tradition tells us this man carried the gospel back to Ethiopia and that nation became a strong Christian nation as a result. His conversion brought Christianity into the power structure of another government.

You can do what Philip did when the Lord asks you. Just listen to the Lord and be obedient. He puts opportunities like this one all around you. Well, you might not go as far as praying with him, but then you might. I was able to pray with the man in first class on the airplane that day. At any rate, you can start. All you have to do is listen, see, and respond. You are the "Philip" of this twenty-first-century.

Something to Consider

Go to the first chapter of the Book of Joshua and count the verses in which Joshua is told to be strong and courageous. How many are there?

Read in 1 Samuel 17 where the Lord used an uneducated, unknown youth to do what was considered an impossible task. Why did this young man succeed? _____

_____

_____

_____

_____

_____

_____

Action Steps

Start today. Be like Philip and go out to find the person or people the Lord has waiting for you. "Be strong and courageous. "Do not be terrified; do not be discouraged, for the LORD your God will be with you wherever you go" (Joshua 1:9).

Start a notebook and fill it with information you need to remember about the new friends you meet.

Plan your next time to see each person you meet.

Add the names of those you meet to your prayer list. Thank God for the divine appointments He gives you.

Chapter 11

Relationships
Are the Key

Laughter is the shortest distance between two people.
—Victor Borge

Relationships, ah, relationships. They are what hold a family together. They are the glue for a congregation. They are the bond for a community. They are the strength of a nation. Relationships. I wonder why we don't give more attention to relationships. We so often just take them for granted. Like they are supposed to just develop because, you know, just because. It really doesn't work that way. Good and precious relationships take conscious effort.

The foundation of Jesus's ministry was relationships. He spent His precious time with those 12 handpicked men and the handful of women that followed Him. The Son of God placed His trust in just these few. They had His time, His attention. They were His agents to carry on His ministry after He returned to heaven. From what I read in the Gospels, they ate the same food, they slept in the same places, and they walked the same roads together. All the while, Jesus was teaching them and listening to them. They had His full attention. They were His focus. He showed them how to live, and they knew it.

Since Jesus placed so much value on relationships, what do you think our assignment is?

From Friendship to Relationship

God uses something very precious to us as a metaphor of our relationship with Him. It is marriage. Christians are His bride. His beloved. What a relationship!

Looking back to the time when my husband-to-be was showing interest in me, I remember that we both were consumed with the process of developing our relationship. We liked to be together as often as possible. Since we were from different parts of the country, we were not like each other. We had to gain an understanding of each other. Talking was important. We developed trust in each other.

After our wedding, our marriage blessed our relationship by enabling it to grow deeper in commitment. We loved to be together, to talk, and to share our day, our time, and our feelings with each other. As time passed, we became more like-minded. Our relationship became more precious every year, and it is still precious to me even though he is now in heaven.

Building friendships with people who are not like you can be the beginning of beautiful, long-lasting relationships. I know. Besides my relationship with my husband, I have spent most of my ministry years developing relationships with those who are not like me, and I find those relationships precious in every sense of the word.

My friendship with a pastor, Enrique, and his wife, Lidia, in Mexico started thirtysome years ago when Enrique asked my husband and me for help through our ministry. That was the beginning. We checked him out. We offered him the help he needed. That was the beginning, and the relationship continued. As his daughters grew up, I became their "American grandmother." When it was time for them to be married, I had a role to play at their weddings.

All because I was challenged to build a relationship with someone different from me.

The Relational Foundation

Relationships are built on meeting needs, developing trust, working on understanding, and learning to communicate with each other. They must develop to the point that we weep with those who weep and rejoice with those who rejoice, as Paul tell us in Romans 12:15.

The relationship Jesus had with His friends Mary, Martha, and Lazarus is an example. They knew Him well. He was a guest in their home. So when Jesus heard of the death of Lazarus, He wept.

I have that kind of relationship with some friends in India and Mexico. At the time of my husband's death, Samuel from India and Enrique from Mexico were with me. A few months afterwards, I was walking in a thick darkness, having lost my husband as my number one cheerleader and not knowing what my ministry was to be without him as my partner. My pastor and friend Claude was there that time to encourage me and pray with me. He too wept with me.

Relationships enable people to encourage each other, to be like Barnabas. Acts 4:36 tells us that Joseph, called Barnabas, was a great encourager for many Christians in the early church. The bricks of encouragement you offer your friends develop over time into a oneness of spirit between you. You are there to help them in their time of need. They are there to help you in your time of need. You are always available to each other—regardless of the inconvenience. Eventually a deep appreciation for each other cements these precious relationships, and prayer seals and reseals them. Who else is going to pray for your friends with the love and understanding that you have? If your friends are not yet Christians, who else in the world will pray for them at all?

On this firm foundation, you can add years of experiences and times of ministry together. Shared laughter and times of celebration. Having fun together and enjoying the journey of life. Making mistakes and laughing them off. Building togetherness with acceptance, communication, understanding, trust, love, and forgiveness. Read on.

How Do You Build a New Relationship?

Bringing new friends into your home, into your comfort zone, will start the process of moving a new friendship into a relationship. Inviting people into your home communicates that they are special. It tells them that you want to know them better. If your new friends are from another country, they may never have been in a typical US home. Coming to your home could be a totally new experience for them, one that makes them feel honored.

Here are some elements that will help move a new relationship to the next level as you entertain your new friends in your home.

• **Acceptance.** Accept your new friends for who they are. Their clothing may not be like yours, but it doesn't matter. Their language may not be like yours. Maybe they have picked up some curse words along the way, but that doesn't need to stop the relationship. They may be too loud or too quiet for your usual taste, but that's OK too. Take them the way they are. Being nonjudgmental is the order of the day.

• **Communication.** To start a conversation, just share with your new friends the things that matter to you. As they look around your home, they will have questions (maybe not verbalized) about your pictures on the wall, the books on your table, and your items on display. Telling them why these things are important to you gives them understanding as to who you are. And talking about your family is always important. They will like to see pictures of your family and hear about each one. In turn, they will want to tell you about their family members. This easy, heart-to-heart conversation brings more interaction. Communicate. Talk. Share.

• **Understanding.** You want to understand. You sense their desire to understand Americans better and to learn what Christianity really is. You know that they have taken a risk by coming to your home, and you honor them for it by showing your desire to understand who they are. As you communicate with them, your understanding of your new friends grows, and they likewise know more about you. They gain some understanding of who you really are, what makes you happy, and what makes you sad. You gain the same understanding about them.

• **Trust.** This element takes more time and more encounters, but it must be developed. You, after all, are the "good Samaritan" and are to be there to help your new friends navigate the highway of life. As they learn to trust you, they will want to know what makes you the kind of person you are. Bringing your experiences with Christ into the picture gives them the answer. As they trust you, they will want to know why He is important to you.

• **Love.** Love is unconditional and sacrificial. As I wrote this section of the book, I had a stretching experience with one of my new friends (he's from Palestine). He was too sick to go to work. I called him, and he told me that his stomach was retching all the time. He didn't have many friends. He didn't have insurance. He needed help. What could I, who have the love of God in my heart, do for him? What better way to develop a relationship than to lovingly provide help? Jesus gave me His example in the story of the good Samaritan, who bound up the wounds and cared for the one whom he found injured along the roadside. It was my turn. So I took him to the hospital.

• **Forgiveness.** Forgiveness comes into any relationship. It is a requirement for moving to the next level. It is a gift that you can be the first one in the relationship to give. By doing so, you model what Jesus would do.

My new Palestinian friend offended me twice. After his surgery, I took him a *Reader's Digest* and a Bible in Arabic. He took the magazine, but he threw the Bible back at me, saying he would just throw it out if I didn't take it. A day later, I told him I was praying for him. His response was, "Don't pray for me. I don't want you to do that. I can die and it's no problem. Just keep your prayers to yourself."

It was up to me to decide whether to be resentful and hurt or to forgive. What would Jesus do? I knew I must forgive. I did, and I waited. Not long after that, he called me and wanted to talk. Great. I had been moving too fast for him. I had been pushing him instead of listening. I needed to slow down and just be there for him. He wasn't ready for prayer. He wasn't ready for information on Christianity. He just wanted a friend, a relationship. I was thankful that he called me, because it gave me a new opportunity to continue with our relationship in spite of my error in rushing him.

You can't win your new friends to Christ without a good relationship. Besides your care, concern, and patience as the relationship develops, you must actively practice acceptance, communication, understanding, trust, love, and forgiveness. Jesus did, and He helps you do it too. After the relationship is established, your new friends will be open to know more about Jesus. They will start asking you questions as they see Jesus in you. You will have earned the right to be heard.

Church and Relationships

So when do you take your new friends to church? That's a good question. Attending a church service may be so strange to them that it won't really help them in their journey to know God. However, it might not hurt to take them sometime so they will know where you go and why you go there. They, in any case, are tiny babes in learning about Jesus and His way.

Don't expect a church to be the teacher. The teaching is up to you. They can learn about Jesus from your life, your example, and it will be more meaningful to them. Taking them to church is not the answer. You are.

I made a mistake one Christmas by taking my Indian friends to my church's Christmas pageant. To me it was the wonderful story of Mary and the birth of Jesus. The music was spectacular. The costumes were beautiful. It was great for our people. But as I sat there in the sanctuary beside my Indian friends, I realized that they didn't have a clue as to what this pageant was all about. It didn't make sense to them. It confused them. Oh, how I wished I had not brought them. I sunk deeper and deeper down in the pew as the story continued. What was being sung and performed was way out of their comprehension. For non-Christians who had never heard about the birth of Jesus, it was weird, beyond their understanding. Yes, it was wonderful for all of us Christians, but not so for those who didn't already know the story.

Some services or crusades go for the big push. Go get them now. Pull in the harvest. Get them on their knees before they get to the exit. This is not what we are talking about. Most of us will never be on the stage in a stadium or even the platform of a church. Instead, we'll be in line at the grocery store or at a table in a Mexican restaurant.

Our job isn't to preach to the multitudes. Ours is to build relationships with kindness and love. Kindness that is consistent. Love that is caring.

Don't get me wrong. I'm not saying that you shouldn't take friends to church. What I am saying is this: Don't let taking them to church replace your responsibility to develop their understanding of what it means to be a Christian. Church comes later.

Culture 101

I can often discover if someone is from the Deep South by the way the person addresses me. That "yes, ma'am" and "no, ma'am" make me feel special even though I know that is just a normal response. But I can't build friendships and relationships with people of other cultures on smiles and light conversation alone. I have to understand where these people are coming from.

I know how to make mistakes. I've learned that well. But with different cultures, I may not even know when I do make a mistake. To build a deeper relationship, I have to understand my new friends' culture. I have to learn how they think, which is not always the same as I do. I have to listen intently and patiently and let them know I love them. As I gain understanding of their culture, I discover what is a blessing and what is offensive.

You can start your Culture 101 education by visiting different ethnic restaurants. At an Indian restaurant, for example, you can sample various dishes and ask the waitress what she likes best. Here is your chance to ask if she is a vegetarian and why. Are all people in India vegetarian, or do some of them eat meat? If the dining room host is from India, you can gain a lot of great information from conversation with him about his country. Are you aware that Muslims don't eat pork? That bit of information is essential when you invite them to your home.

Notice the décor in a Japanese restaurant. How is it different from a Greek restaurant? The smells more pungent perhaps? The clientele, are they mostly from Japan? Why? What are the favorite foods in Japan?

Try Thai, Russian, or Moroccan food. Visit an authentic Chinese restaurant. Mexican too, of course, but look for one owned by Mexicans and preferably in a Mexican neighborhood. How about Irish, Turkish, Vietnamese, Italian, German, French, Korean, and others? Give them all a try. Find out about the people who own or work in these places. Politely ask them to say a few words in their language, like "hello" and "good-bye." At every place you go, don't leave without finding out how they say "Thank you." Write it down so you can say it on your next visit.

As you are talking to people in these different restaurants about their homeland, you will have their undivided attention. Why? Most of them want a relationship with Americans and you are talking with them and about what is near and dear to them. They love it that you are noticing them. You may see how faces actually light up when you start asking questions. They will remember you when you come there again.

Ask about the clothing in their country. How is life different than here? Why did they come here? Check out their likes and dislikes about living in the US. And all the while, think how you would handle moving to their country and making a living there. That would be a bit scary for most of us.

Ask them about the religions in their country and if they practice a religion here. You can find out if there is a festival or special celebration in your city for people from their country. If so, that would be worth going to with your new friends.

As you do this, gaining a Culture 101 education, you will realize anew that the United States is certainly a melting pot of cultures and peoples. Our country is a cultural mosaic. We are as diverse and as varied as a nation can be, yet we all are neighbors.

You will discover that different cultures also have different ways of greeting each other. We usually go for the handshake. In many parts of Asia, the people put their hands together and give a little bow. They bow their head slightly when they ask you something or when they are saying good-bye. In other parts of Asia, it's with a kiss on one cheek or both cheeks—men and women.

There are many other cultural norms for you to discover. In Thailand, the people never cross their legs when seated. It is impolite to have your toe pointing toward someone. In some places in Latin America, the people, to be polite, will try to tell you what you want to hear even if it isn't exactly correct or true. You must always stand in an orderly line in Japan, but not in India. There, it is expected that you must strive to gain the attention of the clerk.

In some countries, women are not supposed to carry on a conversation with a man. In India, the women do not sit down to dinner; they serve and take care of the guests first and then eat later. That practice is so different from our ways, but we need to honor it.

When I was in China, I discovered that where your host seats you at a table has significance. A guest of honor is always seated facing the door and next to the host. Others are seated around the table according to their status.

Don't worry if you don't know all of these things. You can ask your waiter what some of the culture differences are. And you can ask your new friends what is different for them here in America, what we do differently than they do in their birth country.

Life is interesting. We are all different. We all have our own ways of doing things. As you spend time with people from different backgrounds, you'll find your Culture 101 class really gets interesting. And here's an added benefit. After a relationship is formed, you will discover that your new friends will accept your culture (and your mistakes) more readily.

Possibilities

With the eyes of Christ, you see possibilities. They are all around you. Look at your neighbors. Where are they in their relationship with Christ? Every one of them is different. Mine are. My neighbors include a Catholic, a Greek Orthodox, a Jew, a Syrian Orthodox, a Presbyterian, a Methodist, a Disciple of Christ, and a few that don't go to church. How about your neighbors?

With Christ's eyes I see that I have a Chinese neighbor down the street and an Indian neighbor two blocks down. About a half mile away is another Indian family. Possibilities. What do they really know about Jesus? Do they have any understanding of our Heavenly Father? Who will tell them?

What's your assignment?

Something to Consider

After you have made some new acquaintances, respond to the following.

From what countries do your new acquaintances come?

_____

_____

_____

_____

Read up on their cultures and their history. You can find out a lot on the Internet.

List those new friends with whom you feel certain you can build a deeper relationship. _____

_____

_____

_____

_____

Action Steps

Organize a prayer group at church to pray for internationals in your neighborhood. Pray specifically for your new acquaintances.

Invite your new international friends to your home.

Invite some of your other friends to meet them in your home.

Ask your new friends to teach you some of their language. Connect through basic communication. Start with words and phrases such as "thank you," "please," "God bless you," "hello," "good-bye," "how are you?," "I appreciate you," "please be my friend."

Something More to Consider

Relating to Muslim Women

Since 9/11, Islam, terrorism, and predominately Muslim nations, such as Iraq, Iran, Afghanistan, and Saudi Arabia, have dominated the US news. And you've probably realized that people of the Muslim faith are all around you. You may not have noticed them before that dreadful day, but now you do. They are as stunned as you are that those towers fell, that the Pentagon was hit. They are as concerned as you are about the conflicts in the Middle East: the Iraq war, the Israeli-Palestinian conflict.

What are you to do when you see people from a Muslim background at the stores, in the restaurants? Simple. Do what Jesus would do—get acquainted and build a relationship. Invite them into your home. Have them over for dinner. Take them a cake. Cut some flowers from your yard to give to them. Become a friend. Have a servant heart. Help them with any struggles or problems. Be there in troubling times. Be there when times are good. Be there.

The following section is taken from a *Today's Christian Woman* interview by Corrie Cutrer with Ergun and Emir Caner ("The Muslim Next Door," March/April 2004, www.christianitytoday.com). The two brothers are former Muslims who now follow Christ; Ergun is president of Liberty Baptist Theological Seminary in Lynchburg, Virginia, and Emir is dean of The College at Southwestern (TCS) on the campus of Southwestern Baptist Theological Seminary in Fort Worth, Texas. They cowrote *Out of the Crescent Shadows: Leading Muslim Women into the Light of Christ.*

What misconceptions do we have about Muslim women?

Emir: One is that a Muslim woman isn't approachable. A Christian sees a Muslim woman wearing her traditional attire and thinks, I can't speak to her; she's too different.

Ergun: Muslim women also can have misconceptions about American women. Some feel Americans hate them or believe all Muslims desire war. They're cautious of Christianity because they associate it closely with Western culture.... It's important for Christian women to establish friendships to break down these stereotypes.

How can we effectively build relationships with Muslim women?

Ergun: By taking the initiative and extending simple acts of hospitality. Many Muslim women feel isolated in America. They're hungry for fellowship. And Christian women share the same interests and pains Muslim women have—they're both working to raise children, or they both may be far from their families.

Emir: This kind of outreach is key, especially if a Muslim woman recently moved to the US. She doesn't know where to get a driver's license or how to apply for a job. A Christian woman can establish a friendship with her by showing her the ropes in a new community.

Muslims have many misconceptions about God and Jesus. They have no understanding of God's grace and unconditional love. Islam is a works-based religion with requirements to prove allegiance to Allah.

Christians should not fear conversations about religion with their Muslim neighbors. You can share what Jesus has done for you. As Emir Caner said later in the interview:

Many Americans don't realize that in Muslim culture, friendly confrontation and debate are enjoyable. Discussing your faith compassionately with a Muslim while remaining friends shows her your faith is reasonable and defendable.... The "politically correct" idea that all religions are equal isn't a message that leads Muslims to Christ.

Don't worry about seeing your Muslim friends come to Christ immediately. Working with them will take a lot of your time, your prayer, your friendship, and your conversation. Plan on years, but pray for months. Conversion for them is serious. A decision to follow Christ is often a decision to leave their family since Islam strictly forbids conversion. What's critical are the relationship you have established with them and the times you have had to talk about our Abba Father and His wonderful grace.

Chapter 12

Time at Last to Talk

He who refreshes others will himself be refreshed.
—Proverbs 11:25

It is amazing how much someone can discover about Christians without discussing the subject of our faith at all. Remember the song lyrics, "They will know we are Christians by our love"? We are to build relationships first, and then start talking about Jesus. Some people call it *witnessing*. Just what does that mean?

Witnessing is so much more than trying to bring someone to a decision for Christ. As we build our relationships with our new friends, we are witnessing through our life and our actions, which show love and compassion. When the time is right, we can also witness through our words.

As you are in the process of building relationships with your new friends, you can't help but learn what their needs are. Some are lonely, some are guilty, some are angry, and others don't understand that there's more to life than what they have or are seeking.

Study your friends. See what their needs are. Their needs will open the door for you, and meeting their needs will earn you the right to be heard when you talk to them about Jesus.

Where do you begin? What do they already know, and what do you have to be ready to explain?

Talking About Sin

It is appropriate for you to assume that your new friends may know nothing about Jesus, except His name. They may have no concept of the gospel or the good news that is waiting for them. They may know of the Bible but have no understanding of its value. Chances are that your new friends are not familiar with God's point of view about sin and its consequences.

Let's first look at a simple explanation of one of the foundational concepts of our salvation, which is sin. What is sin?

Sin is the inheritance that Adam bestowed on us when He and Eve committed the first sin, disobedience. We all have the desire to sin. It comes to us at birth, and it wants to grow and consume us as we grow. It's like a disease, and without treatment, it keeps spreading.

We must have treatment for our sin. That treatment comes only from Jesus Christ, the most famous person who ever lived on earth. He gave the human race the only treatment for sin that works—His death in places of ours. Because of sin, we will die physically and, without Jesus's treatment, we will die spiritually too. (We'll look more closely at what Jesus has done for us later in this chapter).

The word *sin* means breaking God's laws about right and wrong. God's laws are written in the Bible, and they are also written on our hearts. We all have an innate sense of right and wrong even if we have never read God's laws in the Bible. Doing what is wrong is like committing a crime, and someone must pay the price for it.

A missionary to a tribal group in Ethiopia told me that the people in the remote villages where he is working had never had any contact with the outside world and knew nothing of the Bible, yet they had a code of laws. Their laws were basically the Ten Commandments with the exception of observing the Sabbath. They had a prescribed punishment for those who broke their laws. They also had a plan for forgiveness. In their hearts, they already knew right and wrong.

Sin creates a broken relationship between God and us. When we sin, we are doing the opposite of what He said is the right way to live. We want to be the one to take care of ourselves, and so we set our will against God's.

Sin also destroys relationships with others. We only have to listen to the news to know the evil that people are capable of doing. Sin pushes us to get ahead in life by putting ourselves first, lying, trampling on the rights of others, and even killing to get our own way. In the international scene, sin brings about war, assassinations, and the widespread suffering of innocent people.

Sin is an addiction that we just can't break. We can keep trying and trying, but we just can't overcome the addiction. Paul expresses this condition in Romans 7:15,18–20:

> *I do not understand what I do. For what I want to do I do not do, but what I hate I do....I have the desire to do what is good, but I cannot carry it out. For what I do is not the good I want to do; no, the evil I do not want to do—this I keep on doing. Now if I do what I do not want to do, it is no longer I who do it, but it is sin living in me that does it.*

Based on this explanation, could you communicate what sin is in a conversation with your new friends? A simple "I wonder" statement about the root cause of the wars in the world could lead you into an explanation of your understanding of sin.

Compassion or Tolerance?

As you are walking with Jesus, you are going to discover some twenty-first-century issues. Here is one. Americans are being taught to think in certain ways, ways that our society says are correct. Because of our multicultural society and global economy, for example, we are told to be tolerant of those who are not like us.

Your new friends may ask you about your views on tolerance. Their very lives may challenge you. Be ready.

Tolerance? Is that what Jesus taught? I don't think so. Webster's Dictionary defines *tolerance* as sympathy or indulgence for beliefs or practices differing from or conflicting with one's own. With that definition, we know Jesus had sympathy for the person but never indulged their sinful beliefs or practices. He certainly didn't give in to the values of those around Him.

Is tolerance what Jesus expects of us today? No. Something more, something better. He is our example. Remember, we are following Him and not making our own path. We are His disciples.

He hasn't changed the Ten Commandments or any other part of His Word, telling us that we are to be tolerant of sin. But He does tell us to love the sinner. Obviously, His method is to be our method. He is our teacher. We are His disciples. We learn from Him.

Jesus felt compassion for those in trouble, the sinners, the sick, the downtrodden, the adulterers, and the thieves. Today He would include the gays, the abortionists, the atheists, and the pornographers. He saw people's sins, their problems, their needs, and He had compassion. When they would let him, He changed them. He forgave their sins and healed them of their sicknesses. He showed the better way, the holy way, the way of love. Some accepted. Some didn't. But that didn't stop Him from having compassion, from reaching out.

Didn't He weep over Jerusalem? Wasn't His heart

broken many times? Didn't He get tired of people's complaints when they chose not to change? Yes, yes, and yes. But the choice to respond was always theirs.

The Apostle John says, "For God did not send his Son into the world to condemn the world, but to save the world through him. Whoever believes in him is not condemned" (John 3:17–18).

Condemnation, judgment, rules of the church, unwritten rules of a congregation. These approaches do not bring people to Christ. Only love. Love and compassion.

Condemnation or Love?

Over coffee one day, one of my new friends started telling me how awful she has been. Yes, she had done many things that fell under my definition of sin. She asked me if all of those things were wrong, and she asked why they made her feel so bad. Here was the choice to condemn her or to help her understand and bring her to the Savior.

"Jean," I responded, "the Bible tells us wrong things are sin and that sin is a transgression of God's law. So now we have to know what God's law is. It starts with the Ten Commandments and then goes on to where Jesus tells us to love the Lord our God with all our heart and our neighbors as ourselves. There is the answer, Jean, and the problem. We know to do what is right, but it isn't necessarily what we want to do. Also, sometimes other people can call something a sin but the Bible doesn't. We have to be aware of that too."

"How can you know? Sometimes I don't know what is right, and other times it just doesn't even seem important to me."

There was real anguish in her voice. I waited for a moment to let her know I could sense her pain. When I spoke again, it was with compassion.

"Jean, it goes back to deciding to put Christ first in your heart and life. If you do that, then you will want everything you do to be pleasing to Him. You will start thinking before acting and deciding if what you are considering is right. You will learn to get answers from God's Word too and not just accept what another Christian considers to be sin.

"We have all sinned, but it is up to each one of us to ask the Lord for forgiveness. He will take away our sin and our guilt, and the Bible tells us that He will remember it no more."

Our conversation went on. This was one of those special times when she wanted to know, and I was there to help her find the answers.

Who Is Jesus?

Jesus Himself was asked this question repeatedly. You will probably be asked this question at some point in your friendships, and it will bring you to the reason you want to share Jesus with your friends. Having your thoughts together in words that someone from another culture can understand is important. All of your new friends desperately need this kind of understanding of Jesus. Especially if they feel neglected, uncared-for, or cast aside, then this is the Jesus that they can relate to.

This is the Jesus to talk about.

• **Jesus is the Son of God.** God Almighty is the creator of all, everything. God made the world, and He made mankind. Even before mankind sinned, He planned a way to forgive that sin. That way is through His only Son, Jesus Christ, whom He chose to send to the world on our behalf. Jesus Himself tells us in the Scriptures that He is the Son of God (John 3:16; 10:36).

This is the Jesus who is the Son of Almighty God.

• **Jesus is our deliverer.** Jesus can and does deliver us from sin. We call what He offers us *salvation*. We are saved from the addiction of sin. It is like being born again. He forgives our wrongdoing. He removes our guilt. He is able to do all of this because He is the Son of God, who died for us and rose again, and was sent from heaven to do this for us. He has paid the price for our sin. Jesus frees us from the power of sin, and now we are able to live our lives very differently. He is our victory in this life and our assurance of life after death—an eternity with Him.

This is the Jesus who gives us victory.

• **Jesus is the Good Shepherd.** When Jesus was on earth, He explained who He was in a way that even the simplest, least educated people could understand. He said He was like a shepherd, a good one. In the Bible, John 10:14–15, it is recorded that Jesus said,

> *"I am the good shepherd; I know my sheep and my sheep know me—just as the Father knows me and I know the Father—and I lay down my life for the sheep."*

We are like sheep, and Jesus knows each one of us intimately. He knows our names. He knows our problems. He knows our weaknesses. As our shepherd, He cares for us and protects us. Because we all have sinned, He chose to save us by suffering, dying, and laying down His own life for us.

This is the Jesus who knows us and cares for us.

• **Jesus is our healer.** He saw people and had compassion on them. In the Book of Matthew 11:5, Jesus said,

> *"Go back and report John what you hear and see: the blind receive sight, the lame walk, those who have leprosy are cured, the deaf hear, the dead are raised, and the good news is preached to the poor."*

Jesus healed people physically and also emotionally and spiritually. He understood people and addressed what they needed most. He still does. He still heals and has compassion on us.

Here is a story from my own life about how Jesus heals. Early in 1980, my husband was diagnosed with a heart problem. He was failing fast and unable to keep up his pace. He would have attacks of some sort and be down for a couple of weeks, and then he would get back on his feet until the next one came along. Because of his heart condition, he resigned his position as president of Project Partner with Christ, the missions agency we had founded. At church, people prayed for him. At home, we prayed for his healing too, but he kept getting worse. And we continued praying.

I was scheduled to take a team of pastors to Haiti to do a pastors' conference. I found it so very hard to leave him even for a few hours, let alone a long period of time. He was unable to do very much at all, and his skin had taken on a grey tone. I told him I wasn't going to go, but he insisted that I was supposed to go because the Haitian pastors were expecting us.

Leaving him was hard, but it was only for ten days. I did it.

When I returned, Chuck was waiting for me at the Cincinnati airport. As we started walking to the baggage area, I realized he was walking like his old self. He used to walk fast, but with this heart problem, his pace had become so slow.

"Chuck," I said, "how are you able to walk this fast now? What's going on?"

He turned to me and said, "I'll tell you when we get in the car."

We walked on to the baggage carrousel, where he picked up my two suitcases and, I couldn't believe it, carried them to the car. He hadn't been able to do that for a couple of years.

"Chuck, what's going on?" I repeated. "You couldn't carry those when I left home."

He threw the suitcases into the trunk and turned to me saying, "Donna, I think the Lord has healed me." He went on to tell me what happened. He'd had another one of those attacks. He managed to get to the couch in the living room and lay down. He didn't know how long he lay there, but then he remembered he had been invited out to supper. He felt that he couldn't go, and he knew he should call his friends and tell them that he wasn't coming.

As he got up and started walking toward the phone, he suddenly realized that the pain was gone. He twisted around, assuring himself that there wasn't any pain. He didn't call his friends. Instead, he went over for dinner. The next morning was Sunday. He still felt fine, so he went to church. Each day he felt better and better to the extent that he started doing some of those repair jobs that were needed around the house. He hadn't done anything like that for a long time.

Yes, Chuck was totally healed. The doctors confirmed it. He had been a pilot before and had lost his license to fly due to his heart condition. After his healing, he wanted to fly again, so he started the process with the Federal Aviation Administration (FAA) to get his license reinstated. That took time and numerous medical exams, but in about eight months, the FAA issued his new license.

This was a miracle. His heart was fine. The Lord had healed his heart. The medical profession said it couldn't be done. The Lord was his healer.

This is the Jesus who heals us.

• **Jesus is our friend.** When He was here on earth, He loved to be with people, and He was a friend of ordinary people, people that the religious society called "sinners." He cared for them even if they were prostitutes or tax collectors. He cared for those that were demon possessed or criminals.

Jesus hates sin but loves sinners. He cares for everyone. Think with me for a minute. Jesus, the Son of God, isn't asking us to stand in line to see Him or to pay a tax to talk to Him. He, the Almighty God of the universe, wants to have us as His friends. Do we have any other friends like that?

Speaking of friends, I do have a very special friend who made a decision years ago to go with me on my trips to foreign countries. Mary realized the dangers I encounter while traveling alone, and she made a commitment always to be available to me. She has been with me in China, in India, in Laos, and many other countries. She is such a tremendous blessing because she helps me make choices, recognize dangers, and make decisions. She is a wonderful special friend, and I value her very much.

Jesus is my special friend too. He is always with me in every circumstance, every country, every time, and every situation. He is our best friend, not just an acquaintance. *This is the Jesus who is our friend.*

• **Jesus is our comforter.** He is always with us and always ready to help. He is compassionate. He gives us the assurance to go on in times of trouble. The Bible says that He wept when He found out that His friend Lazarus had died. He understands our problems. He feels our pain. As we talk to Him, we feel His presence and His comfort. We can walk and talk to Him, tell Him our troubles and our pain. He understands, and He surrounds us with His arms of love.

When my husband of 45 years died in 1992, I was devastated. I needed a comforter. I was alone for the first time in my life. The grief was overwhelming. My pastor chose to be a comforter to me. He had the love of God in his heart and the Christ-like compassion I needed. But he is human and he has limitations. Jesus is not limited, and He understands our sorrows. Jesus is always there for us. Always. *This is the Jesus who comforts us.*

Sharing the Gospel

You can share the gospel because you have personally encountered God's love and grace. His love and grace are not a one-time thing. I am sure you have experienced them again and again and again in your own life.

You have developed a relationship and a level of trust with your new friends. You have learned to listen so you can determine where they are hurting. After many times of listening, the time is coming, if it isn't here already, for you to talk more about Jesus, specifically about God's plan of salvation. But no two people are alike. One friend may be ready quite soon, while another may take a year or several years. Learn to recognize God's timing.

Of course, since the beginning you have been praying. You can pray specifically for their hearts to be touched by God and to be eager to hear about Him. Pray that you will know when to share the good news—that they can become God's child by accepting Jesus. You can do it too soon, talking about God before your friends are ready. And you can wait too long to share the gospel and miss the chance entirely.

Here is where the stories of your personal encounters with God plays a big part. Your friends will listen as you tell them what you have experienced and how the Lord has helped you. A canned presentation that is not personal doesn't usually fit their need. Your friends will respond better as you relate your own story and how the Lord has made a difference in your life.

We Christians have picked up a "church" vocabulary. It won't work here. We have to explain words like *sin, saved, redeemed, faith,* and *born again.* Yes, we know what these words mean, but our new friends may not. Avoid using these terms and instead use common words or phrases that they can understand. You may have to explain simply and in more detail what you are talking about instead of using a word they don't understand. Remember, one of my friends misunderstood the word *Christian*, thinking everyone in the United States is a Christian.

This time of sharing what the gospel is and what it means to you needs to be a conversation between the two of you, not you doing all the talking. Make it a normal conversation and not a lecture. A lecture isn't witnessing. And a conversation is not a one-sided sermon. Check your listening skills.

Here might be an opportunity for your friends to sidetrack you onto a controversial issue. This is not the time for that. Set another time for that discussion. Your friends may say something about Christians or Jesus that you disagree with. This is also no time to be defensive. No arguments, please. This is a time to listen to their response, to wait, to love, and just to be there for them.

They may reject you. Can you handle that? Jesus was rejected many times. It will hurt when you are rejected, and you may even think you have failed God. This is not the time to take it personally. Maybe you moved too fast. Maybe you pushed a bit. There will be another time. This time does not seal their destiny eternally. There will be other opportunities.

Sometimes their response is simply nothing. Neither yes nor no. They may want time to think over all that you have been talking about. There will be another day.

Using Prayer

At some point, you may be able to pray with your new friends. Before you do, ask them if you may pray. Ask them what they would like you to ask God in your prayer. Use their names as you are praying. Simple, honest prayers are needed. If they don't want you to pray, that is all right. Remain non-defensive. Sometimes they may be checking out your attitude rather than your answers.

I usually close my prayers with "in Jesus's name." It takes a conscious decision to do this with a new friend who doesn't know Jesus. There are times I talk about praying before I pray, and I can address my use of Jesus's name this way: Everybody understands the need for passwords now because of computer programs. Did you know the Bible has a password about praying? John gives us a clue. I didn't recognize it until recently, but it is there. I often use one of my grandkids' names for a password on the computer, but John's is even better. John 16:23 quotes Jesus, "I tell you the truth, my Father will give you whatever you ask in my name." I now use Jesus's name as my "password" when I go to the Father. As John says, He gives "whatever you ask in my name."

Being an Ambassador

It is quite an honor to be appointed an ambassador. If you were chosen by our President for an ambassadorship, you might be sent to France or Germany or perhaps Mexico. Your purpose would be to represent the United States and answer questions when they come up. You would have opportunities to tell people what our values are and how our countries can work together.

You will probably not be selected for that position with our government, but you have already been selected to be an ambassador for Jesus Christ. It is a very special assignment. It is one in which you are appointed to tell people about Jesus, what His values are, how He can help them, and why He cares. The best part is that everybody has a longing in his heart for just what you have to offer. Christ is without equal in the entire universe. You know that, because of what He has done for you. And you know that He can do unbelievable things for everyone and anyone who believes in Him.

Representing Christ is in a totally different league than being an ambassador for a country. We do not use pressure, and we aren't working on the merit system. We are Christ's representatives here today, and we are to be like Him, to love like Him, to care like He did, and to be there for those who want to find Him.

As an ambassador, you want people to start asking you questions, not pound them with answers to questions they haven't asked. Your task is to take Jesus to people, not people to Jesus. Don't be afraid to direct your conversation to things of eternal value. When the opportunity is right, tell them what the Lord has done for you. Relate your personal story or one of those stories of yours that you have written and practiced. Let them know that you love Jesus.

A wise ambassador knows how and when to talk and when to listen. You want to be with your new friends many times in the future and give them plenty of opportunities to ask you questions. Pray that their heart's desire is turned toward God and that you will be there for them at the right time. It is a rare thing for someone to be ready immediately to accept Christ as Savior, so don't expect it (unless the Lord produces a miracle, which He sometimes does).

You think they may be offended if you talk about what Jesus has done for you? It depends on your smile, your love, and your calm desire to tell them how important Jesus really is. You can tell if they don't want to hear any more, and then you know to stop. (And if they are skeptical, let that be their problem, not yours. Show the love of the Lord. After all, you are His disciple.)

Are They Ready?

How exciting it is when your friends tell you that they have some questions they want to discuss. They might even feel it's time for a change in their life. Or they might be interested in going to a Bible study or to church with you. They might ask you how they can have Jesus in their life as you do. They might express a desire to become a Christian.

This may occur when you expect it, or it may be months and years away. The key is never to give up. You are to continue caring for them until they make a decision for

Christ (or even if they never do) and also after they make that decision. No matter where they are at, they will always want to talk with you and ask more questions and want to know how Christ can help them with their current problems. Take time to listen to them.

Your friends may think they have sinned so much that God could never forgive them. They may simply want to know how to pray to become a Christian. They may expect the Lord to work all kinds of miracles in their life, straightening up their wrongs. It is wonderful that they are asking you questions and wanting to talk. Your guidance, love, and direction can help them make a clear decision for Christ.

When people make a decision to become a Christian, they need coaching. This is a critical time in their growth in the Lord. Ask them if they would like to read the Bible with you. Nurture them. They will want to stay close to you in their growth. Because of you, they are in a new relationship with the Lord, and they simply don't know what to do next. Maybe they would like to join a Bible study group. Try to get them into some small group connected with a church.

This is how the early church grew. This is how the church grows today. It takes time, prayer, commitment, determination, obedience, and your love. Who are the disciples now? You are. I am. We are the ones to take the good news to those who have never heard. Yes, we first look and then we start talking (and listening to their questions, concerns, and problems).

Something to Consider

What is the password? _____ Use it.

Listen intently to your friends to understand better their needs. What are their needs? How can you pray for them?

_____

_____

_____

_____

_____

_____

Action Steps

Write your thoughts on what you need to do to witness more effectively. Put your ideas into practice.

_____

_____

_____

_____

_____

_____

_____

What does Jesus offer us? Write down how you might describe these wonderful blessings to your new friends when you have the opportunity.

_____

_____

_____

_____

_____

_____

_____

Chapter 13

Divine Appointments

But thanks be to God, who always leads us in triumphal procession in Christ and through us spreads everywhere the fragrance of the knowledge of him.
—2 Corinthians 2:14

You were really lucky."
"What a coincidence."
"How in the world did that happen?"

Have you heard those phrases? I have a name for the wonderful opportunities that come to us. I call them "divine appointments."

I claim Jeremiah 29:11, and you can claim it too.

"For I know the plans I have for you" declares the LORD, "plans to prosper you and not to harm you, plans to give you hope and a future."

It is a joy to know that the Lord has His special plans for me.

Looking back over my life, I have seen His plans and how those plans have been revealed to me. As I get older, I have started anticipating His plans and seeing if I can identify them at the time that they are unfolding. Each morning I pray, "Lord, this is your day. What do you have in mind for me today? Lead me according to your plan, and help me to see it and serve you."

I am not the only one who has divine appointments. You have them too. Each of us has to learn to recognize them and use them in serving the Lord and expanding His kingdom.

On an Airplane

She came stumbling down the aisle with two awkward bags. Her seat, the window one, was next to mine. After I moved out of her way and she was seated, she started the conversation. She was on her way to visit some people in Costa Rica that she didn't even know. Her friend in New York had arranged the visit so she could spend a week in that country. She was on the final leg of her trip, and her anxiety was growing.

This was easy. I was sure the Lord had put us together so I could help her, because I had been to Costa Rica several times. As the plane taxied down the runway, she asked me about the plane, about Costa Rica, and about how to go through immigration. She wanted to know what everything would be like there. After I answered her questions, she asked about me.

"I'm a speaker, and I am going to Costa Rica to see some of my friends," I replied.

"Oh, really? What do you speak about?"

"I speak about the purpose of life, as I've discovered many people go through life without ever thinking about their purpose and what they want to contribute," I responded.

"This is great!" she said. "I need to talk with someone about my purpose and what I am supposed to be doing."

Our conversation continued with more questions, which led to her big question, "How can you know the Lord is with you?"

Great! I had hoped she would ask that. We had a marvelous opportunity to talk about the Lord, and I then had the privilege of praying with her right there on the plane.

This encounter and many others like it with strangers have taught me that life is full of opportunities to talk to people about the Lord. I look forward to strangers sitting next to me on planes. I look forward to salespeople coming to my house. Some of these people are very easy to lead into a conversation about their purpose in life. That gives me an opening to talk about God's purpose for our lives, which is to know Him and serve Him.

I pray daily that God will bring people into my life that He has ready for me to help in some way, or even lead to the Lord—to be useful for Him. Divine appointments are planned by the Master of the universe. What a joy to be a part of them.

At a Fast-Food Restaurant

We met at a fast-food restaurant when I was ordering a milk shake. His name was different—Samish.

"Say friend," I started out, "that's an interesting name. Where are you from?"

He looked directly at me as his face broke into a big smile. He stopped and looked at me as if no one else had ever given him that much attention.

"I'm from western Africa," he replied with a big smile.

Not willing to let the conversation stop there, I asked what country.

"Guinea. My family is still over there. I have been here two years now, and I am learning your language."

"I don't know that much about Guinea. What are the religions there?"

"It is nearly all Muslim, and I'm a Muslim."

Our conversation went on until there was a line behind me. That encounter was the beginning of our relationship.

I went back to that restaurant, and each time I saw Samish, I talked with him a little more. I wanted to know him and help him understand the love and grace of Jesus Christ. He had never been in an American home, and his concept of American culture was what he saw on TV, at the movies, and in the newspaper. One day I invited him to my home for dinner, and he accepted.

That night I had prepared a special dinner for Samish and another friend of mine, who was there to help me with the conversation. We would have chicken, since Muslims don't eat pork. I thought we would spend the evening as if we had all the time in the world, talking and enjoying ourselves. All the while, my friend and I would be praying that Samish would want to know our Lord Jesus Christ. The warmth and comfort of my home and the pleasure of sharing a meal together would be the perfect opportunity to talk about the Lord.

Samish was late arriving, which was strange. He explained that he had taken the time to help another employee get home that evening because her car was in the shop. When I called him a "good Samaritan," he wanted to know what that was. Great! My first opportunity to talk about Jesus.

As the evening progressed, we had more and more opportunities. Since he was among friends, he felt free to ask questions. They rolled off his tongue. "Are all Americans Christian? Then how do you know who is and who isn't? What is the difference in all these religious buildings (churches) with different names?"

We talked about the Bible, and I had the *Good News for Modern Man* version ready to give to him.

Meeting Samish isn't a coincidence or luck. It is one of God's divine appointments for me. He gives them to me. It is up to me, as His disciple, to make the most of them.

On a Trip

I just returned from a trip to China with my 15-year-old granddaughter, Morgan. We had one of those divine appointments that the Lord gives. It happened on the morning that Morgan and I took a catamaran up the Pearl River toward Guangzhou.

We found our seats next to a man from Atlanta. He was an engineer for an electronic company and was traveling in numerous countries for two to three weeks at a time. This was his 30th time in China. John, he told me his last name but I couldn't catch it, said that he had two children, Ryan and Nicole, teenagers. He talked to Morgan about the necessity of adequately preparing for college and the importance of good grades in high school, so she could get scholarships. That was excellent advice, and I appreciated it.

John told us that he is a pilot and loves to fly, especially Cessnas. I'm a pilot too, so I told him about flying on a little Cessna that I once had and then later the Convair 240 and the Fairchild 27. These stories moved into why Morgan and I were in China.

He said that he was a Catholic and went to a men's Bible study every Thursday morning, which he said he loved. The group was studying the Book of James at the time. We talked about our relationship with God and that it is more important than which church a person attends. He agreed, and he went on to say that a church could be two or three or four people too, according to the Bible.

His biggest concern, he said, was if his wife and kids were at the gate of heaven with him and St. Peter stopped him from going through because he hadn't done enough. As I told him that salvation was not based on merits, he wanted to hear more. He listened intently when I said that God gives us salvation by grace when we repent, when we ask Him to forgive us and we become His children. John seemed quite relieved to hear that. Yes, that was what he wanted, the assurance of salvation. I suggested that he read the New Testament and pray, telling him he could have that assurance. I shared some Scriptures that came to mind. He was appreciative of our conversation and told me he was going to do that. Yes, he said, it was time for him to do that.

About that time, the trip was over. We parted company, and he went on to his business appointment. But a seed had been planted. I pray that it will grow and bring him the joy of being a child of God.

As I told this story to my small group at home, one of my friends said, "Donna, you can do that, but I don't think the Lord wants me to."

Her response is exactly why I am writing this book. The Great Commission is not just for the first-century disciples and for me. It is the Lord's directive, His command, His commission to all His disciples.

Sure, I am better now at this kind of sharing than a beginner, but I was a beginner myself once and had to learn to recognize divine appointments and move into them with the assurance that they were part of God's plan and He would give me the words to say. This is what it means to be a disciple of Jesus Christ. As we try this, practice, make mistakes, and have successes, He is with us, encouraging us and helping us to see more of the divine appointments that He brings our way.

With a Monk

One day when I was traveling with a missions team in Laos, we divided into teams of two to do a prayerwalk. Liz was my partner as we entered the Wat, the grounds of a large monument and two huge Buddhist temples. Ahead of us was a statue of an ancient warrior king. He sat high above us on his lofty stool with his big hat, a broad smile, arms crossed, sword on his lap, and feet in heavy boots.

Liz and I moved to one of the big ornate temples. No one was around this area. Climbing the 14 steps, we noticed the gigantic red doors were open. As we ventured to look inside, we saw two young novice monks in their orange robes. They were about 25 feet back from the doors. One motioned for us to come in.

Slipping out of our shoes, we gingerly approached the carpet in front of them. One called in English for us to come on up to where they were sitting. Then he motioned for us to sit down on the carpet with them so we could talk. That was interesting. I had never been in a temple like that one, much less had the opportunity to talk to a monk.

He told us his name was Phon, and he was 22 years old. He welcomed us and asked where we were from. The interest increased as we answered, "America." Then Phon and the other monk wanted to know what city. Figuring they knew little about American geography, I simply stated, "Near Chicago."

The conversation continued as we all asked more questions. Phon was the talkative one. He had been a monk for three years. He left his home in southern Laos to be a monk and learn English at the monastery. He told us that he planned to go to the university next and get a degree in computer science and English.

When I got a chance, I said, "We are Christians. Do you know about Christians?" Phon nodded his head yes, so I went on. "Do you know Jesus?"

"No, I don't know Him. Who is He?" Phon answered.

I turned to the other monk and asked him the same question.

"No," he said, "I don't know Him either."

Here was my opportunity.

"Well, the Creator God is in heaven. He made the world, and He made man. He sent His Son, Jesus, to the earth so He could teach us how to live. If we follow His teaching, we become a part of the family of God. This gift is given by God's grace. We don't earn it, and we don't gain merits to get it. It is a beautiful gift to those who believe in Jesus and what He teaches. As a part of God's family, we are also given the gift of eternal life in heaven with Him. We don't earn it, and we don't die and come back to this earth again. When we die, we go to be with Him. Have you ever heard of this?"

"No," Phon said as they both shook their heads.

"That special relationship with God is what makes us Christians. Christians go to church, usually on Sunday, and we sing and pray and worship Him. He gives us peace and joy."

"Is that the only time you go to church?" Phon asked.

"Oh, no. We can go several times during the week."

Our conversation was just what I wanted it to be as we continued. Then he asked where we got our information about God.

"Phon, we get it from our holy book. We have this holy book that gives us our instruction and tells us how to become a child of Almighty God."

They had more questions. Then Phon asked where he could get a holy book. I told him I could send him one if he wanted it in English. That was exactly what he wanted. He reached over for paper and pencil and wrote out his name and address. I later asked an older missionary what to send him, and soon a copy of *Good News for Modern Man* was in the mail to him.

This encounter was in Laos, but it could be repeated with Buddhists here in America. In the US, we have Buddhist temples in our cities, and those who go to them or work in them may want to develop a relationship with an "ordinary" American. How do we help them do that? Just be at the right place at the right time and see what the Lord has ahead.

There are Buddhists here who don't really know who Jesus is and have never seen our holy book. What if the Lord wants you to relate to one of them?

A Surveyor in My Yard

The man walked by my window right beside my house. What was he doing out there this Monday morning? Watching, I saw that he was talking on his cell phone. I looked the other direction and saw the survey truck out in the middle of the intersection. OK, he was a surveyor, but why was he surveying here?

It didn't take me long to open my sliding back door and go around to where he was. Since he appeared to be hiding behind a tree from another man in the street, I asked, "Are you playing peek-a-boo?"

"Hi!" he replied. "No, I'm just talking to the man out there at the truck. We are checking on this lot line. There have been some questions as to whom these trees belong. Looks like they are yours. You like that, don't you?"

"Of course, these trees are important to me. Someone came one day when I wasn't here and cut down three big ones over there, but they were just outside my lot line. I would have tried to stop it if I had been here, but I was gone when it happened."

"You are retired now, and watching this house over here go up?" he asked.

"Oh, I'm not retired. I still work." The word *retired* just isn't in my vocabulary so I always react to that kind of remark.

"Where do you work? What do you do?" he asked.

"I'm a writer, an author, and I write books and stories. Keeps me busy all the time."

"Really. What kind of stories do you write?"

"Christian ones. I'm on my third book now. Got two already published."

"Oh, you have? What are they about?"

I told him, and then I asked, "Are you a Christian?"

"Well, I don't go to church, but I quit drinking a few years ago and I do know the Lord. I haven't been baptized though. I'm afraid of water and not sure the preacher can get me out fast enough. I don't want to drown and go to hell."

"What makes you think you will go to hell? If you are His child and are being obedient to Him, you won't go to hell. Listen. If you had a gun and pulled it out right now and shot me, I know I would go to heaven. Is that assurance or what? Everybody can have that assurance. You can have that assurance. You don't have to worry."

"My grandmother was a good Christian. I'm doing better, but I still smoke. Quit once and then started again."

"It's great that your grandmother was a Christian, but that won't be the way you get into heaven. You have to ask God to be your Father and for you to be His child. Ask Him to forgive you of your sins, and then talk to Him everyday. That's all you have to do. He is just waiting to listen to you."

"Yeah, I know. Yeah, He is my Father. You make it sound easy and good."

"It is! It's as easy as saying, 'Father, forgive me of my sins and let me be your son.' Now that's not hard is it?"

"Yeah, I believe that. You are encouraging me, and I am—I'm going to get your book and read it. What's it called? Where can I get it?"

"It's at the bookstore, but if you get it, you have to come back and tell me what you like and what you would like to challenge me about. Would you do that?"

"Sure. I would like that. I will get it, read it, and I'll be back. What's the name of your book? And what's your name?"

"The book is *Climb Another Mountain,* and it is all about the paths that come in life. God gives you a challenge and you choose your response and then you move on to the next step and first thing you know you have climbed a mountain. My name is Donna Thomas. What is yours?"

"Meddie, M-e-d-d-i-e. Here's my card. It doesn't have my name on it, but my name is Meddie. I'm the head of this team, and we come over here all the time."

For that divine appointment, all I had to do was step out into my own yard.

Your Divine Appointments

Now that you see how divine appointments are a part of the Lord's plans for our lives, you can start looking for them. The first thing to do is anticipate them. Next, recognize these precious encounters when they happen and dive right in. What do you have to lose? Use them to talk about the big picture, the purpose of life, and spiritual relationships. Believe that if God gives you these opportunities, He will help you with your words and answers.

One thing is sure. If you start looking for these special times and are open to the Lord's leading, He will give them to you, you will recognize them, and you will thoroughly enjoy the encounters.

Notice in these stories of mine that most encounters did not develop into a relationship. I will never see that monk named Phon again nor will I see the woman on the plane nor the man in China. But with Samish, I do have the opportunity for a continuing relationship.

Notice, too, that my stories are not all about internationals. Once we are in tune with Him, the Lord doesn't limit us as to whom He will put in our paths. He will give you divine appointments at any time, at any place, with whomever He chooses. Isn't that amazing? I love it. Learn to wake each morning with anticipation as to what the Lord has planned for your day.

Something to Consider

Think back and remember some previous times that could have been God's divine appointments for you. Write them here. _____

_____

_____

_____

Pray today that you will start recognizing your divine appointments and that you can use them in talking about the Lord.

Action Steps

Determine to start writing your stories about these encounters.

Tell your best friends about them as they happen. You will encourage them to start looking for their divine appointments.

Praise the Lord for every time you have one of these opportunities. They remind you that God has His plans for your life and He is always with you.

Chapter 14

The First-Century Example

"One heart setting another on fire."
—St. Augustine

You know how you can miss an event 100 times and then on the 101st time, you wonder where you've been? You know how you can skip over a question, not thinking about it, until all of a sudden it jumps in front of you?

My question is, who followed Paul and Barnabas? Who took over Timothy's work? Who continued the ministry of disciples Peter and John and Andrew and Philip? And in their absence, how did the church continue to grow after these disciples were gone?

A Look at the Early Church

Martyrdom for one's faith was the order of the day in the first century. If you were a Christian in those days, it meant that you put your life on the line. You were willing to die for the Lord. Let me repeat. **To be a Christian meant that you put your life on the line and you were willing to die for the Lord.**

During the first century, Christians were often subject to punishment by humiliation, torture, and death. The Apostle

Paul was martyred in the year 67. James, Stephen, and Peter all were killed because of their obedience to the Lord. John, the disciple Jesus loved, died in exile on the Isle of Patmos in 95.

What happened next? Who continued the work those apostles had been doing? What happened to the church? What happened to the other Christians? Did they all run and hide?

According to sociologist Rodney Stark in his book *Rise of Christianity*, everyone but the rich lived in crowded tenements with only one room for a family. They had no running water, no toilets, and no ventilation. Antioch and similar cities had around 200 people plus their livestock per acre. Also, there was no police or fire department or any help in times of crime or disaster. It was a different world than we can imagine, causing the life expectancy to be around 30 years. If they did allow their girl babies to live, the Romans often married them off when they were around 11 or 12 years old.

The Christianchronicler.com, in the article "First Century Pressure," gives us additional insight into Greco-Roman culture at that time:

- Rome faced serious erosion of family ties.
- Rome trusted a multiplicity of gods.
- Romans expressed an inordinate desire for luxury.
- Human life became cheap.
- Roman society displayed overt sexual deviation and perversion.
- Pornography and perversion in art were common
- Drunkenness became common.
- Government by personality rather than law led Rome into cultic practices.
- Rome placated the masses by paternalism.

So where was the church in all this? According to Stark, in spite of all this the conversion growth rate was exceptional. The believers increased in numbers by about 40 percent every 10 years, he claims. Actually, the wives and mothers were the ones that were reaching their neighbors for the Lord. Church historian Wayne Meeks has referred to evangelism at that time as the "gossiping gospel." These women reached out by their words but more importantly by their lives. They caused the church to grow to over 6 million by the year 300 and 33 million in the next 50 years, Stark writes. He calculates that the number of Christians grew from 2 percent of the population to slightly over 50 percent in that 100-year period (250-350).

Why were people converting to Christianity? It was because the followers of Jesus Christ were different. They shared the love of God. They cared for each other. They loved their children. They honored their marriage. Those early believers also made their homes places of prayer and worship even though they lived in those one-room tenements. We read where ordinary women and men were casting out demons and healing the sick. This certainly caused their neighbors to be curious and want to know this Jesus too. They saw the joy, fulfillment, and happiness of their Christian neighbors.

Around 215 Tertullian wrote, "It is our care of the helpless, our practice of loving-kindness that brands us in the eyes of many of our opponents. 'Only look' they say, 'look how they love one another!'"

It was the ordinary, everyday Christians who were changing the world and bringing the gospel to these ancient cities. It wasn't any clergy, or pastors, or bishops. It was committed, devoted men and women who were filled with the Holy Spirit and ministering to their neighbors, one person at a time. St. Augustine is quoted as saying that the gospel grew by "one heart setting another on fire."

The Blood of Martyrs

Martyrdom was a threat for Christians for almost 300 years. Nero, a Roman emperor whose sanity was questioned, carried out the first major persecution of Christians. Soon, the suffering of Christians became a blood sport popular among the Romans. Christians were taught by the church to respect authority and the law. They offered no rebellion and were ideal citizens. Yet the Roman authorities held that Christians were responsible for the decline in paganism. They were to be killed unless they agreed to sacrifice to Romans gods. They would be set free if they would renounce Christ. The persecution went on, with intensity varying by time and place, for three centuries.

Well-known historian Adolf Harnack put it simply in his 1908 book, *The Mission and Expansion of Christianity in the First Three Centuries,* "Here Christianity and paganism were absolutely opposed. The former burned what the latter adored, and the latter burned Christians as guilty of high treason."

Harnack wrote further, "It was by preaching to the poor, the burdened, and the outcast, by the preaching and practice of love, that Christianity turned the stony, sterile world into a fruitful field for the church. Where no other religion could sow and reap, this religion was enabled to scatter its seed and to secure a harvest."

An apparent miracle witnessed by Emperor Constantine led him to change the status of Christianity in the fourth century. In 313, he and his coemperor Licinius granted Christians the unrestricted right to worship as they desired.

Hearts on Fire with Love

The story of the early church gets worse—or better, depending on how we view it. As if three centuries of persecution were not bad enough, people's lives were also devastated by one epidemic after another. Death was in control and yet the Christians were there, still sharing with their neighbors.

In his article, "Salt of the Empire," Mike Aquilina, vice-president of the St. Paul Center for Biblical Theology, describes what typically happened during an epidemic:

> The first people to leave were usually the doctors. They knew what was coming, and they knew they could do little to prevent it....The next ones to leave were the pagan priests, because they had the means and the freedom to do so.
>
> Ordinary pagan families were encouraged to abandon their homes when family members contracted the plague...to leave the afflicted family member behind to die....
>
> Yet Christians were duty-bound not to abandon the sick. Jesus himself had said that. In caring for the sick, Christians were caring for him.
> —*Touchstone*, May 2004

Read this contemporary account from Dionysius, Bishop of Alexandria, who wrote during the great epidemic in 260:

> Most of our brother Christians showed unbounded love and loyalty, never sparing themselves and thinking only of one another. Heedless of danger, they took charge of the sick, attending their every need and ministering to them in Christ—and with them departed this life serenely happy; for they were infected by others with the disease, drawing on themselves the sickness of their neighbors and cheerfully accepting their pains....Death in this form, the result of great piety and strong faith, seems in every way the equal of martyrdom.

Writing in response to those who were not followers of Christ, Dionysius continues:

> The heathen behaved in the very opposite way. At the first onset of the disease, they pushed the sufferers away and fled from their dearest, throwing them into the roads before they were dead and treated unburied corpses as dirt.

The fact that the Christians took care of the sick cut the death rate by two-thirds, according to Stark. Of course, their neighbors were watching these Christians. They saw how their lives were different, how they cared and loved one another. The Christians were like a family, but they were also treating all their neighbors as brothers and sisters.

The love of God was changing the communities. It was not an organization. It was not a church. It was Christians sharing the special love the Lord Jesus Christ gave them for their neighbors, their friends, and their family. This love is what brought the tremendous growth of the early church in spite of persecution, martyrdom, and devastating epidemics.

Do you believe in miracles? Who you are because of Jesus Christ in your life is a miracle. Who I am because of Christ is a miracle. We must believe that all people can change by the miracle grace of the Lord. When Christians let the *fire in their whole being* dictate their love and concern for their neighbors, those pagan cities became changed places.

The Church

When we say the word *church*, what do we mean? We have all kinds of answers for this question in our culture, but what did the word mean in the early centuries? Early Christians believed that the family was the church, their home was the church, and the kingdom of God began in the church/home.

As the early church, the home expressed love, charity, kindness, peace, goodness, and joy. The pagans saw how the Christians loved one another by the way they behaved towards each other in their homes. Their homes were different, and they expressed love to their neighbors and friends. They were known to live by the love of Jesus and not by rules and regulations.

The early church in the home was a place of prayer. You can imagine why. If the believers were possibly facing martyrdom for their faith, they certainly would want to spend time in prayer. They would probably spend a lot of time in prayer: daily, regularly, routinely. Prayer was essential for Mom and Dad. It was essential to teach the children to pray. It was essential to train new converts. Prayer was an essential part of the early church—and look at the growth record.

The church at home knew that it was "on a mission." The believers knew that they were called by Christ to take the gospel to the world. They knew they were the disciples of their day, their century.

We cannot imagine living in a place like Antioch, that horribly crowded city. Nor can we imagine staying in the middle of an epidemic and in a decaying tenement. Yet what would you as a Christian do? You would do exactly what Jesus told us to do, and that is to love our neighbors and serve them in every circumstance. They need to know who this Jesus is and what He has to give them. You also know that if you don't tell them, they will never know.

Home Check

Time to do a home check. What is your home like? Is it anything like the home church of the early Christians? Does love flow between husband and wife, between siblings? Is prayer essential?

You just might be able to do a bit of serving and sharing with others today. Just a simple meal for a neighbor or cutting the grass for one who is having trouble might be the sort of thing that helps them see your love for those around you.

Now look around you in your city. What do you see? Certain things like divorce, abortion, infanticide, pornography, or homosexual activity cannot be overlooked. For the early church, as it is for us today, sin is sin, and it must be taken to the Father for forgiveness and change. We, like the early Christians, are to hate the sin but to love the sinners. We can share the good news with others that sin can be forgiven and that Christ enables us to live above it.

We, like the first-century disciples and those that followed after them, are to reach out in compassion. We are to be willing to do *whatever* to reach others for Christ.

Whatever? The early Christians were willing to be persecuted, martyred, humiliated, and hated because of their allegiance to Jesus Christ. Many died because they were Christians. Are we as willing to do whatever? It is a question for me to consider seriously. It is a question for you to consider seriously as well.

The disciples of these early centuries did their job in their time. The growth of Christianity was phenomenal because of them. They took over when Peter, Paul, and the first disciples of Christ were gone. They were the disciples in their day.

Whose turn is it now?

Something to Consider

Analyze your home. Is it a "church" like the early Christians had? In what way?

Check your family. Does love prevail through all the problems and situations? What do others see in your family?

Consider the possibility of martyrdom. Could you accept it? Why or why not?

What is the most important value in your life? What is next and what is after that?

Are these values worth dying for? Are they worth living for?

Action Steps

List the ways your family has shown love to your neighbors and to others. What are some new ways you can show love to those around you?

_____

_____

_____

_____

_____

_____

_____

_____

_____

Chapter 15

. . . .
. . . .
. . . .
. . . .

International Students from Everywhere

Be wise in the way you act toward outsiders; make the most of every opportunity. Let your conversation be always full of grace, seasoned with salt, so that you may know how to answer everyone.
—Colossians 4:5–6

. . . .
. . . .
. . . .
. . . .

It's not easy to be a stranger and alone in a foreign city. Place yourself in Tokyo, and you can instantly feel that it is *not like home*. If you've not grown up in Hong Kong or Helsinki or Heidelberg, but go to one of those places to live, it will be strange and different to you. You'll have more questions than answers, and a friendly face will be a welcome sight.

Imagine Moscow or Riyadh. Different. Strange. Another language. New culture. Unfamiliar smells. Traffic patterns with unknown procedures. People rushing by, intent on their plans for the day. Exciting. Challenging. Baffling. Unexpected encounters.

These feelings of strangeness and aloneness are felt all the time in city after city in the United States. Many of the international students who come to US universities feel this way every day.

If you have a university nearby, you have foreign students in your city. If you have foreign students, you have people who don't understand our culture and our lives.

If you have people who don't understand the United States, they need someone to give them a clear picture of who we are.

International students are here to learn. They come to the university to take classes and get a degree. There is much more for them to learn, however, than just academics. With or without our help, they will form opinions, right or wrong. They need to learn the right things about us.

The education of international students in America starts before they ever attend that first class. They see our cities, our buildings, our way of driving, and traffic control. They notice our busyness, our politeness or rudeness, our way of eating, and the time that we allot for it.

Our way of speaking English doesn't match what they have been taught to speak either. Common phases like "you know" or "you know what I mean" or "that's cool" or "it's like" don't make sense to them. Imagine our speed talk such as, "where'd ya go" and "wad ya do?" If they have weak English-speaking skills, they are often treated coldly and ignored. Even trying to make a call on our pay phones is a difficult experience.

When you connect with international students and they know you are a friend, they will be consumed with questions. Why don't American families eat together? What kind of work do you do? How can I get a driver's license? How can I ask a girl for a date in America? Do you go to church *every* Sunday? Isn't that boring? There will be questions about movies and DVDs they have seen.

The grocery stores are overwhelming to internationals too. They'll have tons of questions about food and shopping for food. These questions will arise when they come to your home for dinner. There also will be honest questions about the meaning of life, what is false hope, and eventually, as they come to trust you, why you are a Christian. Are all Americans Christian? How do you know who is a Christian and who isn't?

The World Has Come Here

In 2007, there were nearly 600,000 international students studying in US colleges and universities—with the highest numbers from India (83,000) and mainland China (67,000), according to the Institute of International Education (IIE). Students and visiting scholars from nearly every nation around our globe are right here among us. They seem to blend into the daily rush in our cities, and we don't always see them. They are eager to develop relationships with Americans. They want to see what we are really like.

At the present time, there are 317 leaders of foreign countries who were educated at a university here, according to the US State Department Web site (see page 194). These countries range from Afghanistan to Zambia and everything in between. We can't relate to them, but we can relate to students here now who will be in those roles of leadership in a few years when they return home.

Seeing that I needed to become active and do my part in relating to the internationals among us, I looked up the number of the local university and called to ask if they had any student who would like help with English. They certainly did. I asked for a student from the Middle East, and they gave me the phone number of Abdul from Jordan. That was easy.

I called Abdul, introduced myself, and set a time and place to meet on the campus. Never having been there before, I didn't really know where the building was he suggested. As I was driving around and searching for it, I called his number again. He said, "I'm walking down the street right now, and I have on a white jacket." I was driving right beside him! I parked the car and we went into a coffee shop. It really couldn't get any easier than that.

After getting our coffee, we found a table, and I started our conversation by asking him about his family.

"Abdul, you are from Jordan. Tell me about your family.

I want to know about your mother and dad and your brothers and sisters."

Abdul's father died just before he was born. His parents had been to the United States a couple of times previously. He had a brother and two sisters, and they were all married. Of course, he asked me about my family.

Abdul was a graduate student in nuclear energy. That impressed me. We talked more about his university back home and what it was like. Then he asked me a question.

"Would you mind helping me at the grocery store? There are so many things, and I am having trouble just understanding what everything is."

Of course. I was glad to help him. This was perfect, a good beginning, a good way to develop a relationship.

At a later time with him, I said, "Abdul, the next time we meet, I want you to tell me about Islam, and then I'll tell you about Christianity."

He was open to that. We had some interesting conversation, and he was very open to talking and listening.

It wasn't long before he came to my house for dinner. He was much more interested in the house, what I had, the pictures on the wall, and how I did things than he was in the dinner. That was a couple of years ago, and we developed a great relationship. We had wonderful times together, as I answered his questions, and we talked about Islam and Christianity.

Around the first week in December, I had him over to my house again. He asked questions about Christmas. At least some people in every country know about Christmas, but few really know what it is all about. He wanted to know about the Christmas tree and how we celebrate the holiday. He wondered why we buy so many things and why we give gifts. Then he threw a bombshell.

"There is something I don't understand. Is Santa Claus Jesus's father?"

What a misconception. I was so glad that he felt comfortable asking that question. And I was so glad that I was there to answer it. His question provided the perfect opportunity for me to tell him who Jesus really is and why He came to earth.

Easter brought his questions about the Easter bunny, and again I was able to rid him of all those ideas that have come from the commercialization of our special days. We had other times together and more questions before he returned to Jordan. He wasn't here long, but I know he valued our friendship and appreciated learning about Jesus. I was able to start him in the right direction in understanding Christianity.

International Student Ministry Is Strategic

The people of Saudi Arabia, India, Japan, Russia, China, and other nations are no longer thousands of miles away. Our world has shrunk. The people of these countries are now our neighbors. The United States has become a global community. We, as Christians, cannot consider ministry with internationals as optional. They are here. They need to know about the Lord. They need correct answers to their questions, and we are the ones to be there for them.

Yes, it will require supernatural help from the Lord. But this is the world He has called us to live in, and our ministry can begin in our own backyard. We can have a strategic impact on the world as we reach these students. Here are a few points to consider:

- International students come from more than 170 countries, and many of them come from countries that are closed to missionaries.
- Each international student represents a key to opening a closed door to his or her country.
- All of these students must speak English, at least fairly well, in order to be admitted to a US university. We

don't have to learn a foreign language to talk with them.

- These students are ready and anxious to have American friends. They want to improve their English, and they want to learn about American culture. Most are from large families, and they are looking for relationships here.
- After their education, many of them will return to their home country to be in a position of leadership—just as many former international students from their country have already done.
- As we become the missionary to these students, they can become missionaries to their own home countries, in some cases saving our church's resources and increasing the effectiveness of the gospel cause.
- You can go to http://exchanges.state.gov/education/educationusa/leaders.htm where the US State Department has a list called, "Foreign Students Yesterday World Leaders Today." This is an impressive list.

Deb's Commitment

My friend Deb chose to say yes to God's call to reach out to these students, and she has even joined the staff of a Christian organization called International Students, Inc. Here is one of her stories:

Last fall I took a group of Japanese students to the Grand Canyon. At a 1 A.M. stop on a Colorado mountain summit, we got out of the van to stretch our legs. They wanted to see the stars. Since I grew up on a farm in Iowa, I took this sight for granted, but for these 13 college students used to crowded, urban, Japanese homes, the clear sky with billions of stars was nothing short of spectacular.

Maiko, a new, growing Christian, asked me, "Deb, why did God create so many stars?"

I smiled at such a simple but profound question.

"Hmmm. I think God knew that we would be amazed by even just a thousand stars, but He wanted to show us how extravagant He is, and that He gives us even more than we ever need. That's His personality—abundant with love and gifts that will never run out."

Since that time, Deb has had many more interesting conversations with international students. Halloween is difficult to explain to internationals. Here's another one of her stories:

I was driving a Chinese student to a fellowship dinner when we started talking about this holiday.

Lin asked, "I heard that Halloween is evil. Why do some people think that?"

"Some people think of Halloween as innocent and fun—dressing up and getting candy," I replied. "But, Lin, there are others who celebrate it as a day to honor death in a bad, wicked way. They call evil good and good evil, and they worship the devil. There are many Christians in America who worship one God. He is loving and trustworthy, and He gives life. But the devil is the opposite of that. He is deceitful, lying, and wants to destroy. That's why some Christians may choose not to celebrate Halloween."

"OK, I've heard about that," Lin responded.

"You've heard about what?" I asked.

"What you said ... Chr ... Chris ..."

"Christianity?" I finished her sentence.

"Yes, Christianity. I had a friend in Singapore who was a Christian. She read the Bible to me. She said that Jesus is the only way to God, and that He is God's only Son and that He died for our sins. We go to heaven if we trust in Him. Is this right?"

"Wow. Lin, you are right!"

Then Lin proceeded to ask me several questions about

Christianity. Why did Jesus have to die? Was Jesus God or was He a man? She told me she had seen the movie The Passion of the Christ and cried at the end. It was my turn to ask her a question.

"Lin, do you believe in Jesus?"

"No, I don't have a religion."

"Well, Lin, what is keeping you from believing?"

"For 20 years, my government has said there is no God, so it is hard for me to believe. But Deb, I'd love to read the Bible, and I would like to write some questions to ask you next time we are together."

Deb was able to give Lin a Chinese Bible, but their paths soon separated. When Deb was telling me this story, she remembered that Jesus told us that some must plant, some water, and others harvest. Her final comment was, "I am blessed to be a part of this process. I was privileged to plant the seed. I know the Lord will send someone else to water and harvest, wherever Lin may be."

Ilene's Stories

The church Ilene attends has an outreach ministry to international students. Her first connection with a student was with a young woman from Thailand. Subawa, a Buddhist, came to the United States to learn English.

I invited this young girl to our house for dinner," Ilene told me. "That was the beginning of a true friendship. She came often, and more importantly, we talked a lot on the phone. She had tons of questions and needed advice, as she was trying to understand our culture. She wanted to know about Christianity and how it differed from Buddhism. She wanted to know about the Bible and about Jesus and how He could help her with her life and her problems. She wanted to know about assurance of eternal life. Then one day she told me that she wanted to know this Jesus. She was ready to make a commitment. I had the joy of bringing her to the Lord.

Subawa later transferred to another university and married an American. I had the privilege and honor of attending their wedding. Now they have a son. She stays in touch and sends me pictures of the three of them.

Another time Ilene was asked to help with an older woman from Japan who would only be here in the States for two weeks. Ilene actually let the woman stay in her home, since it was such a short time. The major thing this woman from Japan discovered from that experience was the Christian love and consideration that Ilene shared. She had never known a Christian before.

Phama and Her Students
Keun-hye had just arrived from South Korea when my friend Phama made contact with her.

One of her first requests was that I give her an American name. "So Katie she was, and she has kept that name with her American contacts even after returning to Korea.

I got to spend quite a bit of time with Katie, and when she learned that I was 92 years old, she started calling me 'grandma.' Katie was already a Christian when she arrived. She enjoyed attending church with me and enjoyed being in our Bible study too. Her husband soon became a Christian and was baptized in our church.

My present international conversation partner, Yuko, is from Japan and married to an anesthesiologist. Her two boys, ages three and five, keep her busy, but she spends two hours a week with me. I thoroughly enjoy her. She and her husband and children have attended church with me a few times and have been dinner guests at one of our associate pastor's home. I recently gave her

The Purpose Driven Life *by Rick Warren, and I hope to start conversations about that soon.*

Our strange American words have given good laughs. Charley horse? She wanted to know what charley had to do with the horse. Recently she learned what the word picky *meant. It was fun trying to explain that.*

Yuko is asking questions about Christianity—something new to her. Who is this Jesus, and how can He be God? She, like other internationals, wants to know how she can know who is a Christian and who isn't. Having little knowledge about Jesus and God, she is filled with questions. So far, the Lord has supplied my answers for her.

Find a Student

It's really quite simple to find an international student. The hardest part may be finding your phone book and locating the number of the university. When you call, ask for Student Affairs or for the International Student Office. Tell the person you speak with that you want to help a student with English. Soon you will have a name and number. Then the rest is up to you.

Expand this ministry with your friends. Some churches have developed programs for international students. If yours hasn't, you might start and develop your own group. Why not? Pray about it, and then get started. Yes, it takes time. Certainly, it takes energy. But there are opportunities to share the gospel with the world right in your own living room. Remember, you are a twenty-first-century disciple of Jesus Christ.

Something to Consider

Pray that the Lord will give you just the student He wants you to befriend.

Pray about how your church can be involved with international student ministry.

List two or three of your friends whom you will ask to join you in this ministry.

_____

_____

Action Steps

Have you heard about International Students, Inc. (www. isionline.org) or The Association of Christians Ministering Among Internationals (www.acmi-network.org)? These ministries' purpose is to get international students into Christian homes so they can learn about the gospel. They are there to help Christians like you connect with international students and become their friend. Their commitment is to help students adapt in our country and also to help them learn the value of knowing Jesus Christ. Check out their Web sites. Write out the opportunities you see.

_____

_____

_____

_____

_____

_____

_____

Make that call to the university, and set the time for your first meeting.

Chapter 16

Decision Time!

"By this all men will know that you are my disciples."
—John 13:35

It is great to read a good book, go to a strategic class, or attend an exceptional conference. You are inspired and challenged. In the pages of this book, you have been given a vision, taught some practical skills, and you can now envision the results. In any great encounter of ideas, there is always a time when you have to decide if you are going to get started and do all that you have been learning about. That time is now.

It was at this point in my relationship with my friend Pamela that she agreed to go with me to see if she could "first look and then start talking." I chose a Mexican restaurant that was a couple of miles down the road from our church. Not too many people were there that afternoon. Good. I didn't want her to be overwhelmed.

We were led to a table, and then Alondra, a lovely Hispanic woman, came to serve us. We greeted her first with our Spanish words, *"Buenas tardes."* Although Alondra had been in the United States for six years, her English was limited.

When Alondra brought us our drinks, we asked her what was going on in her life here in Indiana. She was not only ready to answer, but she was more than eager to talk with us. It wasn't long before she pulled her cell phone out of her pocket so she could show us pictures of her daughters, Karen and Sophia. I watched as Pamela responded. She was quickly developing a friendship with Alondra and enjoying every moment of it.

When our plates loaded with Mexican specialties came, Pamela asked Alondra if she went anywhere to church. Her answer was no, but she told us she had received some help from a Christian agency. Our conversation continued between courses of nachos and enchiladas.

On leaving, Pamela realized she had grasped the joy of developing a new friendship, a friendship with someone not like her, from another country. She experienced how easy it was simply to choose a restaurant or business, see a person of another culture or even her own culture, and start a conversation that could develop into something more. She saw the possibilities in the future of leading this young woman to know the Lord. Pamela saw how easy it really was, and she left there knowing she would be going back to see her new friend Alondra soon.

The people you see may not be Hispanic or Arab or Chinese, though they might be. Nationality or race really doesn't matter. What does matter is that you look at them with the eyes of Christ and with His compassion to see if you can be of help to them. I heard this slogan the other day, and I have it pasted on my cupboard door. "Think globally, Act locally."

Now it is your turn. It is your eyes the Lord is directing. It is your heart that He has filled with compassion. Being His disciple in the twenty-first century comes more easily now, because your heart is full of appreciation for what the Lord has done for you and confidence that He wants you to reach out, as He did, to those around Him. Yes, God has chosen to use you to *"declare his glory among the nations"* (Psalm 96:3). You can greet each morning looking forward to how the Lord will use you that very day and what divine appointments He has waiting just for you.

- Pray each morning that God will use you and show you how to see people through His eyes. "OK, Lord, what do you have in store for me today?"
- Purposely greet everyone you encounter.
- Notice each person's name and comment on it. "That's an interesting name. Where are you from?"
- When you hear an accent that is not the same as yours, simply ask, "How long have you lived here?"
- Inquire about the person's family and whether they are living in your state or the United States.
- Ask what the person does in his or her free time or when not working.
- Whether the person is from another country or not, there is a time to ask about his or her life purpose. This question gets the person thinking and often responding with more questions. You might go on with the question, "When you are 80 years old, what do think you might wish you had done?"
- When you leave a place where you've just met someone, write down the person's name and the day's date so you can be in contact soon.
- Pray for your new friends daily.

I know about planting a seed, watering it, and watching it grow. Here's a recent email from a friend I received on the topic:

How about this miracle? God says, "If you plant the seed, I will make the tree." Wow, you can't have a better arrangement than that. First, it gives God the tough end of the deal. What if you had to make a tree? That would keep you up late at night trying to figure out how. God says, "No, leave the miracle part to me. I've got the seed, the soil, the sunshine, the rain, and the seasons. I'm God, and all this miracles stuff is easy for me. I have reserved something very special for you—you are to plant the seed."

You, an ordinary Christian, can make a difference for the kingdom of God in your corner of the world, in your community. No, Peter, James, John, and Paul aren't here today. You are. It's decision time. **Go and make disciples of all nations,** and start with the first person you see.

New Hope® Publishers is a division of WMU®, an international organization that challenges Christian believers to understand and be radically involved in God's mission. For more information about WMU, go to www.wmu.com. More information about New Hope books may be found at www. newhopepublishers.com. New Hope books may be purchased at your local bookstore.

Missional Living Resources
from New Hope

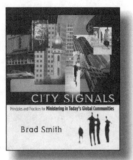

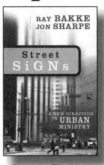

City Signals
Principles and Practices for Ministering in Today's Global Communities
Brad Smith
ISBN: 1-59669-045-3

Street Signs
A New Direction in Urban Ministry
Ray Bakke and Jon Sharpe
ISBN: 1-59669-004-6

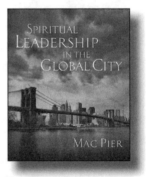

Compelled by Love
The Most Excellent Way to Missional Living
Ed Stetzer and Philip Nation
ISBN: 1-59669-227-8

Spiritual Leadership in the Global City
Mac Pier
ISBN: 1-59669-241-3

Available in bookstores everywhere

For information about these books or any New Hope product, visit www.newhopepublishers.com.